Comments on other *Amazing Stories* from readers ᴀ _ /iewers

"Tightly written volumes filled with lots of wit and humour about famous and infamous Canadians."
Eric Shackleton, *The Globe and Mail*

"The heightened sense of drama and intrigue, combined with a good dose of human interest is what sets Amazing Stories *apart."*
Pamela Klaffke, *Calgary Herald*

"This is popular history as it should be... For this price, buy two and give one to a friend."
Terry Cook, a reader from Ottawa, on **Rebel Women**

"Glasner creates the moment of the explosion itself in graphic detail...she builds detail upon gruesome detail to create a convincingly authentic picture."
Peggy McKinnon, *The Sunday Herald,* on **The Halifax Explosion**

"It was wonderful...I found I could not put it down. I was sorry when it was completed."
Dorothy F. from Manitoba on **Marie-Anne Lagimodière**

"Stories are rich in description, and bristle with a clever, stylish realness."
Mark Weber, *Central Alberta Advisor,* on **Ghost Town Stories II**

"A compelling read. Bertin...has selected only the most intriguing tales, which she narrates with a wealth of detail."
Joyce Glasner, *New Brunswick Reader,* on **Strange Events**

"The resulting book is one readers will want to share with all the women in their lives."
Lynn Martel, *Rocky Mountain Outlook,* on **Women Explorers**

GREATEST GREY CUPS

AMAZING STORIES®

GREATEST GREY CUPS

The Best of Canadian Football

SPORTS

by Graham Kelly

PUBLISHED BY ALTITUDE PUBLISHING CANADA LTD.
1500 Railway Avenue, Canmore, Alberta T1W 1P6
www.altitudepublishing.com
www.amazingstories.ca
1-800-957-6888

Extreme care has been taken to ensure that all information presented in
this book is accurate and up to date. Neither the author nor the
publisher can be held responsible for any errors.

Publisher	Stephen Hutchings
Associate Publisher	Kara Turner
Editors	Melanie Jones & Gaul Veinotte

We acknowledge the financial support of the Government
of Canada through the Book Publishing Industry Development
Program (BPIDP) for our publishing activities.

Altitude GreenTree Program
Altitude Publishing will plant twice as many trees as were used
in the manufacturing of this product.

Library and Archives Canada Cataloguing in Publication
Kelly, Graham, 1942-
  Greatest Grey Cups / Graham Kelly.

(Amazing Stories)
ISBN 1-55439-056-7

  1. Grey Cup (Football)--History. 2. Canadian Football League-
History. 3. Canadian football--History. I. Title. II. Series: Amazing stories
(Calgary, Alta.)

GV948.K435 2005   796.335'648   C2005-905228-7

Printed and bound in Canada by Friesens
2 4 6 8 9 7 5 3 1

To my wonderful grandchildren,
Kassidy, Russell, and Kaitland

Contents

Prologue

The fourth Earl Grey and governor-general of Canada, Albert Henry George Grey, was 58 when he donated Canada's most famous sporting trophy. His birth at St. James's Palace in London, England, in November of 1851, was a harbinger of things to come, since most Grey Cup games are played around that date. In fact, the game has been played eight times on his birthday, November 28.

Grey served as governor-general from 1904 to 1911, a period of strained relations between his government and that of Sir Wilfred Laurier. He was a charming diplomat and a genuine friend of Canadian interests. Known more as a patron of the arts — particularly music and drama — than a sportsman, he probably never saw a Canadian football game, despite the fact its greatest prize carries his name.

The Grey Cup has been forgotten in a basement, lost, found, stolen, recovered, and was almost burnt beyond recognition in a 1947 fire at the Toronto Rowing Club. The original resides in the Canadian Football Hall of Fame in Hamilton. The Canadian Football League, like the Cup awarded annually to its champion, has also been at death's door more times than one can count. But, against all odds, the CFL continues to entertain and enthral Canadians from coast to coast. The league was able to survive its greatest crises and live through its darkest moments because of the Grey Cup game, Canada's single most popular sporting event.

Chapter 1
Grey Cup 2004:
Toronto vs. B.C.

I n 1872, Harry O'Brien started the Toronto Argonaut Rowing Club, named after the crew of the legendary Greek hero, Jason, who sailed the good ship *Argo* in search of the Golden Fleece. To honour the contestants in the Henley Regatta, O'Brian chose the light and dark blue colours of Oxford and Cambridge Universities. The following year, in order to give the membership something to do during the autumn months, the rowing club fielded a group of gridders, called the Argonauts, naturally, sometimes nicknamed the Scullers or Boatmen and also sporting the double blue. Ever since, the inhabitants of Hogtown have thrilled to the exploits of the Big Train, Lionel Conacher, Annis Stukus, Red Storey, Joe Krol and Royal Copeland, dubbed the Gold Dust Twins, Dick Shatto, Jim Stillwagon, Mel Profit, Joe

Theismann, Bill Symons, Don Moen, Matt Dunigan, Derrell Mitchell, Doug Flutie, Paul Masotti, Pinball Clemons, and, of course, Damon Allen.

Teams from Toronto have competed for the Grey Cup 34 times, winning it on 22 occasions, the most in Canadian football history. The first was played on December 4, 1909, between the Toronto Parkdales and the University of Toronto, Varsity winning 26-6 before 3807 fans. The earliest appearance of the Argonauts in the national classic was 1911, a 14-7 loss to the university; their first win a 14-2 triumph over that same varsity team in 1914. The latest appearance of the team wearing double blue took place in 2004 at Ottawa before over 50,000 fans, in some ways the most unlikely Argo Grey Cup of them all.

The great Argo champions of the past were expected to win. The 2004 edition was, to say the least, somewhat of a surprise, despite the eternal optimism of head coach Michael "Pollyanna Pinball" Clemons. Although new owners were committed to winning and the brilliant Kent Austin came over from Ottawa as the offensive coordinator, Derrell Mitchell, who set the single season reception record with 160 catches in 1998, had signed with Edmonton, and the talented and expensive running back, John Avery, back from the NFL, was hobbled by injuries. And, of course, quarterback Damon Allen would turn 41 on July 29.

Winning the 2005 Grey Cup looked like an impossible dream.

Grey Cup 2004: Toronto vs. B.C.

But the Pinball was used to long odds, overcoming adversity, and proving people wrong. Born Michael Lutrel Clemons on January 15, 1965, to an unwed teenage mother in racially segregated Dunedin, Florida, the young man's life revolved around home, school, church, and especially athletics. He excelled at football from the age of eight and always believed it would be his ticket out of the Projects to a better life. Most people scoffed at him because in grade 12 he was only 5 feet 6 inches and 170 lbs. But no one could question the size of his heart. Upon high school graduation, he had offers from institutions as diverse as Morningside College in Sioux City, Iowa, to Harvard and Columbia. He settled on William and Mary in Williamsburg, Virginia, because it was close to home. He would have no way of knowing that decision would dictate the course of his adult life.

After a distinguished college career, Clemons was drafted in the eighth round by the Kansas City Chiefs, who gave him a contract worth $60,000, as well as an $18,500 signing bonus. He silenced a legion of naysayers by making the NFL team as a punt returner. But the '87 regular season was interrupted by a players' strike. Later, Clemons sustained a deep thigh bruise that would keep him out for the rest of the season. Knowing he would have to prove himself all over again the following year, he worked extremely hard during the off-season to be in the best physical and mental shape of his young life. The day before camp opened, the Chiefs' personnel director, Whitey Duvall, called him in for a little chat.

"Mike," Duvall began. "I was one of the guys who brought you here. I know you've had some injuries, but I know you can play. You're our best punt returner, our best running back in terms of hands." Clemons nodded along with everything Whitey said, but he wasn't prepared for what came next. "The club is paying some other guys more money, and they have to figure that into their calculations. It's easier to get you out the door right now, without anybody noticing. If we delay, and you start to practise, the club's concerned that they won't be able to justify releasing you. We don't want to cut you at the end of camp because you wouldn't have a chance to go anywhere else." Clemons was getting the axe before he even suited up for training camp. "You're going to be picked up," Whitey assured him. "There are teams that are interested in you already. I hate that this has happened. It's just part of the game." Stunned and mortally disappointed, Michael Clemons left the office.

A week later, Whitey's assertion came true. Clemons was picked up by the Tampa Bay Buccaneers close to his Florida hometown. But, after only 10 days, coach Ray Perkins cut him in favour of younger players, strange news for 23-year-old Pinball. On the street and without offers, he went back to school and finished his degree. In March of 1989, the Calgary Stampeders offered him a contract. He let the offer lie for a couple of months before finally agreeing to a deal. He was scheduled to report a week into training camp, when, in the Stamps' intra-squad game, their quarterback, Erik Kramer, tore up his knee. The club would have to bring in someone else at that position and forego signing a running back. Again it looked like Clemons' football days were over.

Not so. It just so happened, Ralph Sazio, the president of the Toronto Argonauts, was an alumnus of William and Mary. He invited Clemons to camp.

Michael "Pinball" Clemons would star for 12 years for the double blue. He set a dozen team records and still holds the career CFL mark for all-purpose yards and most combined yards for a single season. Three times a Grey Cup champion, four times an All-Star, he won the Most Outstanding Player award in 1990. Along the way, he became one of the most beloved sports figures in Toronto, even though the city was indifferent to a team they considered minor league.

In September, 2000, the Argos were the laughingstock of the CFL, with an eccentric absentee owner, a coach right out of a grade B prison camp movie and a 1-6-1 record. In an unprecedented move, hoping to cash in on his popularity, the club invited Clemons to retire as a player and immediately assume the duties of head coach. Although they were 6-4 the rest of the way, they missed the playoffs. Pinball moved into the front office when they missed post-season play again the following year. When his sideline successor, Gary Etcheverry, went 4-8, Clemons returned to the bench as head coach, leading the Argos to three playoff appearances and a date with the B.C. Lions in the 2004 Grey Cup.

His coaching counterpart, Wally Buono, was also no

stranger to adversity. After a marvellous career as head coach of the Stampeders, Buono was unceremoniously run out of Calgary by Michael Feterik, an owner from California who wanted to call the shots and play his son at quarterback.

The two coaches had a bit of a history. Buono's first season as head coach of the Lions ended in Toronto's SkyDome, when Pinball's Argonauts beat them in the 2003 crossover playoff game. Before the 2004 Grey Cup, Buono had publicly criticized Clemons — akin to "dissing" Mother Teresa — for resting his veterans late in the season rather than going all out to win a game.

Comparing coaching records, Buono's regular season record of 177 wins was second only to Don Matthews' 213 (going into the 2005 season) and 141 more than Pinball's own track record. Buono coached the Stampeders to three Grey Cup victories in six tries; this would be Clemon's first Grey Cup as a coach. Pinball could be the first black coach to win the Cup. And Buono was one of only three Canadians who had coached teams to Grey Cup championships in the modern era. The others were Les Lear for Calgary in 1948 and Cal Murphy for Winnipeg in 1984.

At 39, Michael Clemons was the youngest head coach in the CFL. His quarterback, Damon Allen, age 41, was the oldest player. While wearing Argo blue, Allen became the most prolific passer in CFL history. He led his team to the Eastern Final the year before, bowing out in the first quarter with an injured hand. On August 12, 2004, Allen went down with a broken leg. Out for the season? Career over? Not Old Man River. Surprising everyone but himself, he made a miraculous recovery, coming back to lead his team into the playoffs and on to the Grey Cup.

Damon Allen was the Rodney Dangerfield of Canadian football, never getting the respect he deserved. Despite all the records he set, he never made All-Canadian, nor was he ever nominated by his own division for the coveted Most Outstanding Player Award. The only honours to come his way were Conference All-Star in 1991 and 1999. At family reunions, he had to forfeit the limelight to his big brother Marcus, a running back who had been inducted into the NFL Hall of Fame.

But Allen's Grey Cup history was impressive. He came to Edmonton from Cal State-Fullerton in 1986, appearing in his first Grey Cup that year behind Matt Dunigan, a 39-15 loss to Hamilton. The following season he came off the bench to lead the Esks to a thrilling 38-36 Cup victory over Toronto. After stints in the nation's capitol and Steeltown, he rejoined the Eskimos and won the 1993 Grey Cup against Winnipeg, 33-23. His third national title came seven years later when he quarterbacked B.C. to a 28-26 victory over Montreal. Going into the match-up with the Lions in Ottawa, Damon Allen was undefeated as a starter in the big game.

Shortly after arriving in B.C., early in 2003, Wally Buono signed the incumbent quarterback Allen to a long-term contract. But, when his former Calgary pivot, Dave Dickenson, became available, he signed him as well and then traded the veteran Allen to Toronto during the pre-season. Buono had been humiliated by Michael Feterik. He, in turn, humiliated Allen, who dearly wanted redemption in the 92nd Grey Cup. Allen was sure Buono would take him to the big dance, but they'd meet again, albeit on opposite sides of the field.

Dave Dickenson also hungered for respect. Slight of build, he had been told all his life he was too small. After setting numerous records at C.M. Russell High School in Great Falls, Montana, he was ignored by the NCAA power-houses and went to play at the University of Montana, where he became an academic All-American and set 26 school records and three NCAA marks. He won 27 out of 30 games, two Big Sky Conference championships, the Division 1-AA Championship and the Walter Payton Award as the outstanding player at that level of college competition.

When he got no offers from the NFL, he signed as a free agent with the Calgary Stampeders to back up quarterback Jeff Garcia.

In 1998, Calgary won their fourth Grey Cup championship with Dickenson coming in to hold for field goals and extra points. The following year, Dickenson became the starting quarterback and played 15 games, despite a severe shoulder injury that hampered his play in the 1999 Grey Cup, a 32-21 loss to Hamilton. After winning the 2000 CFL Most Outstanding Player Award, Dickenson decided to try his luck in the NFL, but after stops in San Diego, Seattle, Miami, and

Detroit, he returned to Canada, a sadder but wiser man. He had an excellent season in 2003, but once again the injury bug struck him down so he couldn't see duty in post-season play. His knee was slow to heal during the off-season, and he was replaced for much of the 2004 campaign by second-year man Casey Printers, who went on to win the Most Outstanding Player Award.

Resigned to riding the pine throughout most of 2004 and desperate to prove he could win a national championship on his own, the pundits were stunned when Buono benched Printers. It was the match-up of the season with the oft-injured University of Montana Grizzly Grad Dickenson and the grizzled powerhouse Damon Allen.

The teams split their season series with B.C. winning 31-10 in Vancouver and losing 22-16 at the SkyDome. B.C. led the league in points, touchdowns, total offence, and passing yardage. They were second on the ground, with Antonio Warren picking up 1136 yards rushing. Lions quarterbacks threw the fewest interceptions, 12, and B.C. had the second best giveaway-takeaway ratio in the league, +16. Toronto's mark was +1, a deceptive figure since Allen had been picked off only once before he was injured on August 12. Toronto ranked dead last in passing because of Allen's injury and the ineffectiveness of back-up Michael Bishop.

Although commentators credited the Argos with an elite defence, the statistics didn't bear that out. They were seventh in giving up yardage. The worst in the league against the run, it was no surprise that Warren ran for 160 yards against them on Grey Cup day. The Argos were third against the pass, had the fourth most interceptions, and were fifth in sacks. But they gave up the fewest touchdowns, indicative of a defence that bent but didn't break. They would have their hands full with Dave Dickenson, a brilliant tactician and passer, and the league's Most Outstanding Player, Casey Printers.

It didn't look good for the Argos.

Toronto lost the coin toss, and Noel Prefontaine's kick-off was returned 15 yards by Antonio Warren to the B.C. 38. Buono's risky QB choice was looking good when Dickenson completed his first five passes in a row, marching the west-erners 60 yards to the Argo 12. Dickenson then rolled to his right and spotted Jason Clermont wide open at the back of the end zone. It was touchdown B.C. at 4:01.

After the kickoff, it was three-and-out for the Argos. B.C. scrimmaged at their 34. Warren lost three yards, Toronto was called for offside, and Dickenson threw incomplete. Duncan O'Mahony went back to punt. The usually reliable kicker shanked the ball a dismal 16 yards! Was this a case of first quarter nerves or a disturbing sign of things to come?

Determined to convert this golden opportunity into points, Allen led his offence onto the field and scrimmaged at the enemy 52. He threw a screen pass to John Avery and then ran for five. Avery carried for eight yards to the 32. After an incomplete pass, Toronto lined up for a field goal try. After being penalized 5 yards, Prefontaine missed from 44 yards out. Argo hopes rose when Lions return man Aaron Lockett ran it out to the two rather than concede a single point in favour of better field position.

Reminiscent of Casey Printers, Dickenson ran for nine yards on the first down. Mixing his plays brilliantly, Dickenson led the Lions from the shadow of his goal post to the Toronto 43. With an opportunity to pin the Argos deep on the final play of the opening quarter, O'Mahony got off a pathetic punt of only 22 yards. Clemons looked up to the heavens and thanked the Lord for his good fortune.

Argo futility continued into the second quarter, with Toronto going nowhere on two possessions. B.C. started out on their 51. Warren slashed off tackle for 14 yards to the Toronto 45. Dickenson overthrew his receiver, and it was third down at the Toronto 45 and an opportunity for O'Mahony to redeem himself and kick the Argos in deep. This punt was even worse, a mere nine yards. Once again, Toronto had wriggled off the hook. Damon Allen then woke up, and the Argo offence came to life.

From his 36, Allen threw to Andre Talbot for 19 yards, Tony Miles for 11, and R. Jay Soward for 24. After two incompletes, Prefontaine got Toronto on the scoreboard with a 27-yard field goal. Four plays later, Allen was at it again. With passes of 35 and 20 yards to Robert Baker and an interference call on Da'Shann Austin, the Argos were at the B.C. one yard line. Allen plunged into the end zone. The convert was good.

B.C. struck back with a field goal to tie. Then, with 1:47

left in the half, Allen completed four of five passes, including a 23-yard strike to Baker in the end zone. After falling behind by 10 points, the underdogs led by 7 at the half.

The Lions led in most categories, including time of possession, first downs, and rushing. A key statistic: Noel Prefontaine was out-punting B.C.'s Duncan O'Mahony 43 yards a kick to 22.8, allowing Toronto to win the battle for field position.

To start the second half, Wally Buono opted for the short kickoff. It worked, but the Lions were offside. Arland Bruce III returned the ensuing kickoff to the Lion 54. Allen completed four straight passes for 43 yards to the Lion 11. John Avery ran for seven and three yards to the one, setting Allen up for his second touchdown of the game. Toronto led 24-10.

Antonio Warren returned the Argo kickoff 19 yards. He then carried the ball five times for 33 yards and caught a pass for eight, and O'Mahony nailed a 37-yard field goal. Toronto 24, B.C. 13.

Toronto started at their 33. With five minutes left in the third quarter, Allen ran for 10 yards before being slammed to the turf by linebacker Carl Kidd. "He's down! He's down!" voices called through the suddenly hushed crowd attending the 92nd Grey Cup at Ottawa's Frank Clair Stadium. Allen was holding his hamstring and grimacing in pain. Trainer Erin Brooks brought comfort and a skilled pair of hands. A few minutes later, she helped the old warrior to the bench. At 41 years of age, it looked like the 20-year football veteran and grandfather was at the end of a distinguished career in the Canadian Football League.

With Allen on the bench, the cats from the Coast had a new life.

The Lions opened the fourth quarter with the ball on their 13-yard line. Western spirits soared when Dickenson engineered a brilliant 98-yard drive: two long passes to Lyle Green, followed by Antonio Warren running 36 and 15 yards to bring the ball to the Argo seven. At 6:06, Dickenson ran into the end zone. Buono decided to go for the two-point convert. Even if it was successful, they would still need a touchdown to take the lead. After two time-count violations because they lined up incorrectly, Buono gave up and sent Duncan O'Mahony out to kick the extra point. Nothing if not consistent, he was wide right. The score remained Toronto 24, B.C. 19. Still, with Damon Allen on the bench, it seemed only a matter of time before the revitalized Lions would surge into the lead.

But as Toronto scrimmaged at the 49, a great roar went up from the crowd. Damon Allen had taken the field!

On his first play back, Allen was incomplete before hitting Robert Baker for 14 yards and a first down at the B.C. 47. When the drive stalled, Prefontaine punted the ball away. Trailing by 6, Dickenson scrimmaged at his 20. On first down, he was called for procedure. Starting over again at the 15, Antonio Warren ran for his last seven yards of the ball game. With second and eight, Dickenson dropped back to pass, lobbing a beautiful tight spiral through the November night right into the outstretched hands of a streaking Geroy Simon. "Oh no!" groaned 52,000 fans as the ball slipped through his fingers. It could have been an 88-yard pass, an almost certain run for a touchdown and a two-point B.C. lead. It was not to be. O'Mahony blew yet another punt, and Toronto took over at the Lion 45. Six plays later, Argo Prefontaine added insult to injury with a 16-yard field goal.

The final score was Toronto 27, B.C. 19.

It was a strange game in many ways. Antonio Warren's 160 yards rushing was the second best performance in Grey Cup history. (Johnny Bright had 171 for Edmonton when they beat Montreal in 1956, 50-27.) The usually dependable Duncan O'Mahony had a miserable day punting, averaging only 27.9 yards. A well-disciplined team during the regular season, the Lions had aggression penalties galore. "The bad penalties, bad kicking, bad decisions hurt us. You can't make those kind of mistakes against a good team," said Wally Buono.

And the Argos were a good team, led by a quarterback who showed why he is one of the greatest athletes the CFL has ever seen. He had just won his fourth ring and his second Grey Cup MVP Award. As Vicki Hall of the *Edmonton Journal* pointed out, "Allen was Damon of old, not old Damon Allen."

After it was all over, the man of the hour said, "It is satisfying, when all year they talk about how old you are. I had the opportunity to show that I can still play on a given day in a Grey Cup game. Through history, great players always perform in big games. If you want to be a great player, the championship is the ultimate game."

Mr. Allen? Your rocking chair is ready in the Hall of Fame.

Chapter 2
Grey Cup 1948:
Calgary vs. Ottawa

The Grey Cup has been more that just a football game for many, many years. Now a week-long festival of dancing, pancake breakfasts, parades, and parties in the host city, Canadians have Calgary to thank. The first Grey Cup festival turned old Hogtown on its ear in 1948, when Calgarians stormed Toronto with chuckwagons, cowboys, Indians and horses, flapjack-flipping at City Hall, and horses ridden right into the lobby of the Royal York Hotel. Since then the smaller cities in the league have added their own flavour to the big event. But it all began in 1948 when Calgarians rode the rails down east for their first-ever crack at winning a Grey Cup.

It was a train trip they would never forget. Whistle-stopping through cities and towns all the way to Union

Grey Cup 1948: Calgary vs. Ottawa

Station in Toronto, the Grey Cup Special picked up steam and turned the game into Canada's premier sporting event. While the players were sequestered in their cars, wives and girlfriends partied around the clock. When the train stopped for any extended period of time, they would bribe the conductor to hold the train up a little longer so they could send somebody to the liquor store to replenish the rapidly dwindling stock. When they pulled into Toronto's Union Station they headed for the hotels, while the team was bussed to the Pig 'n' Whistle in Oakville. After the game, this time with the players, they partied back to Calgary, the only hitch in the proceedings coming when they let the horses out in Medicine Hat to answer the call of nature and it took three hours to round them up.

Player Dave Berry recalled, "Wives went along, but the guys couldn't even talk to them until coming home. Once the game was over, the rules were out the door. That was wild and woolly. But before that, no fooling around. You bunked with the team and you ate with the team and you stayed with the team. You didn't go running around looking for your wife or anybody else." Every time the train stopped, the Calgary Stampeders got off the train and did calisthenics. In one town, that meant sprinting the length of the train through four feet of snow until the conductor called, "All aboard!"

Fifty-five Grey Cups have been played since 1948, with the Stampeders making it to the party they invented 11 times. In the 60-year history of the red and white, success came in three distinct waves, the first soon after their creation, when they represented the West in Toronto in 1948-49. The second was between 1960 and 1971 when they made it to the national classic three times, making the playoffs 11 out of 12 years. The third was from 1991 to 2001, with eight first place finishes and three Grey Cup victories in six trips to the big game.

Senior football began in Calgary in 1909 when the Calgary Tigers joined the Alberta Rugby Union. The team was called the Calgary Canucks during World War I, and the 50th Battalion team formed in 1923. The Tigers were reprised from 1928-1931, succeeded by the Altomahs and the Bronks. The Calgary Stampeders were born on September 29, 1945.

Former Regina Roughrider great Dean Griffing was Calgary's first head coach. Under his direction, the Stamps finished first in 1946 and second in 1947, both times losing the Western Final to Winnipeg. He was succeeded the following year by the notorious Les Lear, who had been in four Grey Cups with Winnipeg. The first Canadian to star in the National Football League, Lear signed with Calgary for $8000 a year.

Rather than fill his American quota with downy-cheeked collegians, Lear chose gnarly old pros: quarterback Keith Spaith, centre Chuck Anderson, receiver Woody Strode, and tackle John Aguirre. Lear picked up homebrew Winnipeg veterans Bert Iannone, Norm Hill, Harry Hood, and Fritzie Hanson. Former Blue Bomber Dave Berry had signed with the team right after the war.

Grey Cup 1948: Calgary vs. Ottawa

"I played for Winnipeg," Berry explained, "but when I came back after the war, there was no place for my mother and father to live. I bumped into [Paul] Pappy Rowe and Dean Griffing, and I told them the circumstances. They said if I decided to play with them, they'd get me a house. I said, 'You get me the house and I'll play for you.'"

While he enjoyed playing for Griffing, he had reservations about Les Lear. "He was rough and tough, but he was unfortunately a little dirty. He expected us to be the same way. If I passed Lear on the street, I wouldn't say hello to him, but if I found out he was putting on a coaching clinic a hundred miles away, I'd be the first guy there."

But Lear knew what he was doing. He transformed the way the game was played by using a four-man line on defence. Before that, eight or ten men were on the line, and once the running back broke through, he was gone. By using a four-man front and three linebackers, a team was able to have a second line of defence against the run, more players to cover the pass, and a variety of ways to confuse the opposition. "When we pulled it against Ottawa," Berry recalled, "one of their linemen said, 'Where the hell are the rest of your guys?' I said, 'Come on through and you'll find them.'"

The Stampeders have always been a passing team, laying claim to some of the best quarterbacks in the business: Frankie Albert, Eddie LeBaron, Eagle Day, Peter Liske, Jerry Keeling, Danny Barrett, Doug Flutie, Jeff Garcia, Dave Dickenson, and Henry Burris. Lear began that tradition with Keith Spaith and

Woody Strode in the late 1940s. The other (Western) teams really hadn't seen a passing game like Lear's. The typical strategy was usually a 60-40 split between running and passing. Most teams designed their defences to stop the run and were ill-equipped to deal with Calgary's new all-out passing attack.

In 1948, the Stampeders went undefeated during the regular season, a record no other CFL team has equalled. The team was a mix of veterans and rookies, including rookie halfback Pete Thodas. A star with the Vancouver Merolomas junior team, a friend recommended him to the Stampeders. Still, it took a twist of fate to give Thodas a 10-year career in professional football. Thodas was on his way to work in a logging camp in northern B.C. and, the night before leaving, he went out with the boys for a last party. He woke up late and missed the boat up to camp. Then the phone rang. Off he went to Calgary.

In addition to his halfback duties, Thodas played defensive back and returned kickoffs and punts. He set a record for kickoff returns of 816 yards in 1952, including 219 yards against Winnipeg on October 5. "Once you were on the field, you never left it. That's the way it was in those days. For the Grey Cup that year we were allowed to dress 19 people. There wasn't a lot of substitution."

The Stampeders certainly weren't down east on a holiday. They were sequestered away in Oakville and trained at Appleby College. They were on the field at 8:30 in the morning, and worked out until 11. They had lunch until 1:30 and worked again until 4. Lear was paranoid and meticulous. "God, it was funny," recalls Pete Thodas. "Les Lear wouldn't allow planes to fly over our practice. He took us down to the basement in this school and he closed all the doors. The team was all down there and he brought out film of an Ottawa game and we watched it. In those days, you either didn't have film or weren't allowed to have film, I don't know which. Anyhow, we watched the film, and, in particular, we watched how Ottawa liked to pull that sleeper play." Ottawa's sleeper play would soon become their worst nightmare.

On Friday afternoon, the team was bussed in and stayed at the Royal York. The streets were packed with horses and chuckwagons, and the players flipped pancakes to get the fans riled up. The Royal York's lobby was cleared out of furniture after fans had ridden their horses right through it. There's still a sign in the lobby of the venerable hotel prohibiting equestrian sports on the premises.

Come game day, Saturday, November 27, the temperature was a balmy 6° C. The Ottawa Rough Riders, coached by Wally Masters, had finished atop the Big Four with a record of 10-2 and had beaten Montreal and the ORFU champion Hamilton Tigers to get to their fifth Grey Cup. The Rough Riders had yet to beat a Western team in Grey Cup competition, but were still heavily favoured. Before the game began, Lear's message to his players was simple: Play your game, play your position, and don't get too many stupid penalties. That's all. Do it right and you'll win. Do it wrong and you'll lose.

Late in the first half, the Stampeders gave the Riders a dose of their own medicine. With a minute left in the first half, Spaith and Strode combined on a pass play to the Ottawa 14-yard line. Left halfback Pete Thodas got back in the huddle to find his left end, Norm Hill, missing. "Where the hell's Norm?" Thodas asked left tackle, Johnny Aguirre, Aguirre grabbed Thodas, growling, "Get your ass in the end position." He pulled Thodas to where Hill would normally be. Thodas said, "What's going on?" "He's out there sleeping it," Aguirre said, nodding toward the sidelines. Thodas shook his head, "You've got to be joking." Stampeder Norm Hill lay on the ground by the sideline. The ball was snapped and Hill headed straight for the end zone. He was ready and waiting when Spaith lobbed the pass from 14 yards out. The ball hit Hill's hands and bounced in the air. A Rider defensive back barrelled into him, knocking him flat on his back. The ball popped up and then fell in his lap for the touchdown.

Tony Golab kicked a single for Ottawa, making the score 6-1 for the West at the half. (Touchdowns were worth five points then.)

In the third quarter, Rough Rider quarterback Bob Paffrath plunged over to give his team a 7-6 lead. Soon after, he threw an overhand lateral pass to Pete Karpuk. It landed wide. Karpuk let it lie, thinking it was incomplete. Calgary's Woody Strode took advantage of Karpuk's lapse in judgment, picked it up, and headed for the goal line.

Said Thodas, "Woody picked it up, started running,

and lateralled it to Michener. I'm right beside Michener and I'm telling him to lateral it to me, but he swallowed it at the 10-yard line. Then they called an off-tackle play and I went across. I met Pete Karpuk on the goal line with the best straight arm I ever threw."

The final score was Calgary 12, Ottawa 7.

Woodrow Wilson Woolvine Strode was raised in Los Angeles by his Blackfoot mother and African-American father. An All-American at UCLA, he became the first black star of the National Football League. His college teammate Jackie Robinson would be the first black player in major league baseball. Both suffered enormous abuse, and when Les Lear asked him to come to Canada, Strode readily agreed. Later, he became the first black television wrestling star and acted in several movies.

And so the Calgary Stampeders won their first Grey Cup. They returned to the big game the following year, losing 28-15 on a field of slush and ice to the Montreal Alouettes. They wouldn't return to the Grey Cup for another 19 years or win it until 1971. Normie Kwong, in the meantime, was traded to Edmonton in 1951, where he starred for ten years and won three Grey Cups. The first victory came in 1954, when once again a controversial lateral pass determined the outcome of the game.

Chapter 3
Grey Cup 1954:
Edmonton vs.
Montreal

One of the most successful franchises in the history of professional sport has been the Edmonton Eskimos. Since re-entering the Western Conference in 1949, the Eskimos have been the dominant force in Canadian football, making the playoffs 49 times in 56 years, appearing in the Western final on 36 occasions, and winning the Grey Cup 12 times in 23 tries. They haven't missed post-season play since 1971.

In 1921, the Eskimos were the first team from the West to challenge for the Grey Cup, losing 23-0 to the Argonauts. Under the name Elks, they returned the following year, bowing to Queen's University 13-1.

It would be 30 years before an Edmonton team

competed for the national championship again. During that time, the Eskimos had an on-again, off-again history, folding after losing the Alberta Rugby Championship to Calgary in 1924, emerging again in 1928. In 1930, Edmonton's team was called the Boosters. They wore blue and white and played in a brand new facility called Clarke Stadium. The Boosters folded after one season and were reborn in 1938 for two years as the Eskimos. They returned to the Western Conference for good in 1949.

The reborn Eskimos were assembled by former sports writer and Toronto coach, Annis Stukus. After the 1951 season, Stukus returned to his sports writing job with the Toronto Star. He was succeeded by Frank Filchock, who got the team to the 1952 Grey Cup, a 21-11 loss to Toronto. Before boarding the plane for the flight down East, Filchock told the Eskimo directors he wouldn't go if he didn't get a raise. He got the raise, but when he came back, they fired him. He was replaced for a season by Darrell Royal, who quit in favour of Frank "Pop" Ivy. During the off-season, Johnny Bright, Jackie Parker, Earl Lindley, Roger Nelson, and Bernie Faloney signed on with the green and gold. Nine members of that 1954 team are in the Canadian Football Hall of Fame. The makings of the first Eskimo dynasty were in place.

One of the greatest Grey cup performers of all time was Normie Kwong, who went on to become Alberta's Lieutenant-Governor and one of the owners of the NHL Calgary Flames. Kwong was a Calgary native and the son of a grocer. He signed with the Calgary Stampeders and played in the 1948 and '49 Grey Cups. He was traded to the Eskimos in 1951 for Reg Clarkson, who didn't last a season. Kwong lasted 10 with Edmonton. Called the China Clipper, Kwong was the greatest Canadian running back in CFL history.

Rollie Miles is regarded as one of the all-time greats on both offensive and defensive teams. He came to Regina in 1951 to play baseball. Although aware of his chops on a football field, the Roughriders weren't interested in signing him, because he was black. A more tolerant attitude and bad weather landed him in Edmonton. Annis Stukus signed him.

"Miles came out to practice, and I took a look at him and thought, this guy's been around a football field once or twice", Stuckus remembers. "I signed him. After five games, I tore it up and signed him to a three-year contract for a lot more money. I knew I had something. He was a great athlete."

During his distinguished 11-year career, Miles was a Western All-Star eight times, three at running back, three at defensive back, and twice at linebacker. In 1954, he made the All-Star team on both sides of the ball. He played in five Grey Cup games, winning three. He was elected to the Hall of Fame in 1980. Regarded as the most versatile player in the history of Canadian football, in 1953 he was denied the coveted Schenley Award for Most Outstanding Player. Instead, it went to his teammate Billy Vessels, an All-American fullback from Tulsa. Vessels was white.

James Dickenson Parker was a native of Knoxville,

Tennessee. He was known in college as the "Fast Freight From Mississippi State" and in the pros as "Old Spaghetti Legs" because of his bowlegged running style. But this football hero could thank his mother that he was able to play any sports at all. At the age of 13, Parker was afflicted with a flesh-eating disease that threatened his entire leg, let alone a career in pro football. "It was a bad time," Parker said. "I went to the doctor every three days and he would cut into my leg. I was in terrible pain. The doctor wanted to amputate it but my mother wouldn't let him, thank goodness." After only one year of high school ball, he had such a distinguished career at Mississippi State that he was inducted into the U.S. College Football Hall of Fame. Upon graduation, the All-American signed with the Eskimos. After retiring as a player, Parker became the coach and general manager of both the B.C. Lions and the Edmonton Eskimos.

One of the best all-round athletes in history, anywhere, anytime, Johnny Bright first came to the CFL with Calgary in 1952. A native of Fort Wayne, Indiana, Bright was all-state champion in high school football, basketball, and track. He set 20 records at Drake University in Iowa, played pro basketball with the Harlem Globetrotters, pitched a no-hit game in the World Professional Fastball Tournament, was an All-American football player, the MVP of the East-West Shrine Game for college seniors, and the first draft choice of the NFL Philadelphia Eagles.

His upbringing in an Indiana slum shaped his life. "In

the ghetto, you hung around the street corner and you went out and mugged somebody or you stole at night. Somehow, that wasn't my cup of tea, and I knew that even at the age of 10 or 11. As far as the gang I ran with, I put certain limitations on what I could get involved in. It became very disheartening because I was ostracized by a lot of guys because I wanted an education. I learned the lesson of being able to be down, kicked, and come back and try again and keep a little self-pride and self-dignity and go on and win."

He came by that the hard way. At Drake, Bright was the victim of one of the ugliest racial incidents in the history of American collegiate sports. He was the first black to play in a football game against the Oklahoma Sooners. The Sooners expressed their resentment by deliberately smashing his jaw. Because there were no hospitals in Oklahoma that would admit a black person, he had to endure an all-night train ride back to Des Moines, Iowa, before he could receive treatment. A photographer won a Pulitzer Prize for his picture of the incident.

While Edmonton was building on a base of U.S. college stars and old Canadian war horses, their 1954 Grey Cup opponent, the Montreal Alouettes, loaded up on veterans from the American pro-ranks.

Montreal was an original member of the Interprovincial Union or Big Four, which was organized in 1907, although football had been played in that city at McGill University since 1868. In 1931, as the Amateur Athletic Association

Grey Cup 1954: Edmonton vs. Montreal

Winged Wheelers, Montreal played and won their first Grey Cup, defeating the Regina Roughriders 22-0. That year was the beginning of legal forward passing in CFL ball. Montreal's Warren Stevens threw the first-ever Grey Cup touchdown pass to Kenny Grant.

Torontonians Lew Hayman and financial backer Eric Craddock created the Alouettes in 1946. In their inaugural season, they finished first, but lost the Eastern final to Toronto, 12-6.

Three years later, led by quarterback Frank Filchock (banned from the NFL for failing to report a bribe attempt), seven-time All-Star Herb Trawick, and Virgil Wagner, the Als beat Calgary in the 1949 Grey Cup 28-15. Montreal then missed the playoffs the next three years, falling to 2-10 in 1952. The team turned around with Douglas "Peahead" Walker from Wake Forest as coach, along with stars Sam Etcheverry, Red O'Quinn, Tex Coulter, Doug McNichol, and Alex Webster. In 1954, with receiver Hal Patterson on board, Montreal finished first and went on to meet the Eskimos in the Grey Cup, the first of ten times the two teams would meet to decide the CFL championship.

Pundits regarded the 1954 Montreal Alouettes as one of the greatest football teams ever assembled anywhere. They characterized the Edmonton Eskimos as just another wannabe from the West who would be given a sound thrashing and sent back to the hinterland with their collective tails between their legs. Dubbed a "nickle and dime team" that had no business being on the field with the Montreal Alouettes, Edmonton had their work cut out for them.

The teams took the field on a warm, dry November 27 in Toronto. They would put on a tremendous offensive display featuring some of the greatest players the game has ever known, with the Als setting the still-standing record of 656 yards total offence.

But Edmonton struck first. Quarterback Bernie Faloney marched his team sixty yards to the Alouette three. Rollie Miles took a pitch-out from Faloney and ran to his left on a pass-or-run option play. Rollie wanted to pass. The Als chased him back to the 28-yard line. After Eskie Bob Dean wiped out Herb Trawick with a devastating block, Miles threw to Earl Loindley in the end zone. The convert was good. Edmonton led 6-0.

Receiver Red O'Quinn responded for Montreal, running the pass from Sam Etcheverry 90 yards for a touchdown, a record that stood until 2002.

The Alouettes were known for a play called a flare pass. The quarterback would take the ball from the centre, jump up in the air, and throw a quick slant across the middle between the linebackers to the receiver. The Esks were well aware of the Als' favourite weapon and had seen the films. Eskimo defenders Rollie Miles and Jackie Parker tried to intercept, but they overplayed it, moving too far down field. O'Quinn shot through, stretched out his hand, and the ball stuck. The red-head was off and running. Miles and Parker gave chase, but it was too late. O'Quinn was at the goal line before they had a chance to catch him. O'Quinn put on one of the greatest performances in Grey Cup history that November day, catching 13 passes for 316 yards, both records yet to be broken.

Later in the opening quarter, the Eskimos regained the lead with a Bob Dean field goal before Bernie Faloney capped an 85-yard drive with a touchdown, pushed into the end zone by Normie Kwong. The Westerners were ahead 14 to 6. But their spirits fell just as fast. Centre Eagle Keys was carried off the field on a stretcher with a broken leg.

Montreal kicked it up a notch with touchdown drives of 100 and 90 yards. The first one ended with a Red O'Quinn touchdown, the second was scored by halfback Chuck Hunsinger on a pitch-out. The score at the half was Montreal 18, Edmonton 14. Montreal had the momentum.

The only point scored in the third quarter was an Alouette single. But, early in the final quarter, Sam Etcheverry connected with Joey Pal on a 14-yard touchdown strike. A few minutes later, Bruce Coulter intercepted for the Eastern champs who proceeded to drive the ball down to the Eskimo seven. At the three, Montreal coach Peahead Walker opted to go for it on third down. Edmonton held. Inspired by the defence and led by the brilliant play of halfback Glenn Lippman, the Eskimos roared back for a touchdown. With less than three minutes to play, the underdogs had closed the gap to five points. The score was 25-20.

Rather than try to run out the clock, Montreal's

The Edmonton Eskimos play against the
Montreal Alouettes, Toronto, 1954

Etcheverry wanted to score again and put the game out of
reach. Mixing his plays like a magician, he led his charges
to the Eskimo 10. Back in the huddle, he called Chuck
Hunsinger's number.

Over the years a few great or controversial plays stand
out as crucial in determining the outcome of a Grey Cup
game. In 1954, it was the Hunsinger play.

Chuck Hunsinger was an Alouette halfback. The
ball came to him off the snap and, under pressure, things
went awry. Jim Staton missed his block on the tackle and
Edmonton's Rollie Prather and Ted Tully came barrelling

44

through. Hunsinger panicked and tried to throw it forward to guard Ray Cicia. It didn't work. He jumped in the air and was smashed by Prather and Tully. The ball came free and Eskimo Jackie Parker came through like a shot, scooping it up and running 90 yards for the touchdown to tie the game at 25. It is one of the most disputed plays in Canadian football, with the Alouettes swearing it was an incomplete pass and the officials saying it was a fumble.

Jackie Parker, one of the greatest offensive performers in U.S. college and Canadian football history, is best remembered for that defensive play in the 1954 Grey Cup. Parker recalled what happened. "They were trying an end run, and Rollie Prather and Ted Tully got through and hit Hunsinger simultaneously. The ball popped out and I happened to be there. I picked it up and started running."

Red O'Quinn looked back on that fateful day and recalled, "I was on the bus going from the Royal York out to the stadium and I was sitting beside Chuck Hunsinger. Everyone was so keyed up about the game. Chuck was sitting beside me and said, 'The only thing I don't want is to be a goat. I don't want to mess up.'" It turned out to be the biggest mess-up of his career. Today he laughs about it, saying, "If it hadn't been for that play, I'd have been long forgotten."

Successful place-kicking is the result of precision developed through hours of practice and game situations. The centre must get the ball seven yards back into the holder's hands with the laces such the ball can be placed without a major adjustment. Before the ball is caught, the kicker is moving forward. Split-second timing is everything. Change part of the equation and a simple task becomes difficult. That was the situation faced by the Edmonton Eskimos who had tied the score at 25.

Parker's 90-yard run tied it up, but it was up to kicker Bob Dean to break the tie with the extra point. Dean hadn't missed all year, but with the loss of centre Eagle Keys who broke his leg early in the second quarter, it would be tough. A study in courage, Keys had limped onto the field to snap the ball for a Bob Dean field goal and two converts. By the time Parker made his dramatic run, Keys could not continue.

A switch this late in the game was more than disconcerting, but in the huddle the boys were ready. "Let's not mess up," someone said. "No mistakes." Replacement centre Bill Briggs snapped the ball. It went straight back for Bob Dean's kick. He put it straight though the uprights to win Edmonton's very first Grey Cup championship, 26-25.

The Eskimos went on to make it three straight Grey Cup wins over Montreal with convincing wins in 1955 and '56. Normie Kwong retired after Edmonton lost the Grey Cup to Ottawa 16-6 in 1960. Miles called it a day in '61, Bright two years later. Jackie Parker was traded to Toronto in '63, the same season Eskimo head coach Eagle Keys was fired. It was the end of an era.

Chapter 4
Grey Cup 1962: Winnipeg vs. Hamilton

One of the great rivalries in Canadian sport has featured the Hamilton Tiger-Cats and the Winnipeg Blue Bombers. Known simply as the Winnipegs, the representatives from the Red River city won the West's first Grey Cup in 1935 at the expense of the Tigers, right in Hamilton. They would meet as the R.C.A.F. Bombers and Hamilton Flying Wildcats before settling on the names they go by today.

Hamilton teams have appeared in the Grey Cup 29 times, winning on 15 occasions. Winnipeggers have cheered their boys on to victory 10 out of 22 tries. Between 1957 and '65, the Cats and Blue Bombers faced each other in the big game six times. The clubs hooked up in some of the strangest

Grey Cup games ever played, but none stranger than the one they called the Fog Bowl.

"Neither snow nor rain nor heat nor gloom of night stays these couriers from the swift completion of their appointed rounds," wrote the Greek historian Herodotus in the 5th century B.C. Nowhere did he mention fog.

At 9° C, that December 1 game was the second-warmest Grey Cup ever played in Toronto. Fans filed into the Canadian National Exhibition Stadium, sporting sunglasses and light attire, prepared to enjoy a great football game on a balmy afternoon. Although there had been some mention of such a possibility, the fans were blissfully unaware that several miles south of the CNE toward Niagara Falls, a combination of warm air and cool water had created a fog that was creeping inexorably toward the 50th playing of the Grey Cup.

Befitting the golden anniversary of the Grey Cup, the 1962 game featured spectacular play by both sides. Hamilton opened the scoring when Garney Henley took the ball from quarterback Joe Zuger at his 36. Henley wove through the entire Winnipeg defence 74 yards for a major, still the second-longest touchdown romp in Grey Cup history.

The Bombers replied with a long drive to the Ticat 17 and a killer play by the Lincoln Locomotive, Leo Lewis. Winnipeg's Hal Ledyard handed off to Lewis, who rolled to his right and threw a touchdown strike to fullback Charlie "Choo Choo" Shephard. Amid the action, a chill settled over the lakefront, and wisps of fog had begun to steal into the stadium.

Hamilton's offence struck back with Joe Zuger completing two passes and running twice, getting the ball to the three-yard line. Bobby Kuntz barrelled into the end zone. Shortly after, Hamilton recovered a Bomber fumble at the Winnipeg 18. Garney Henley ran the reverse for the touchdown, and Hamilton was up by five.

Winnipeg soon jumped back into the lead. Hal Ledyard completed three passes to the Hamilton 35. He then threw to Farrell Funston near the sideline. He flipped the ball to Leo Lewis who went roaring by untouched to pay dirt. The score at half-time was Winnipeg 21, Hamilton 19.

By half-time, the CNE was engulfed in fog. Most of the spectators couldn't see the tremendous action on the field, and CFL Commissioner Sydney Halter went down to the sideline to check the visibility. He ordered half-time shortened by five minutes and told head referee Paul Dojack to move the game along as quickly as possible.

The visibility was so bad, the players could hear the ball being kicked, but they couldn't see it. "All of a sudden you'd hear it hit the ground beside you," Sutherin recalled. "You'd run over to pick it up and you could see bodies coming at you, but you could only see them from the knees down. It was scary." But spectacular plays were still the order of the day in the third quarter. First, Garney Henley completed a 53-yard drive to the Winnipeg 15. Zuger threw to Dave Viti for the score, moving the Cats into a five-point lead. Leo Lewis quickly answered back with a 64-yard kickoff return. A few plays later, Charlie Shephard ran in for the major. Gerry James converted. At the end of three quarters of play, shrouded in a fog that would have made Londoners feel at home, it was Winnipeg 28, Hamilton 26.

Dojack was uneasy. "We knew ahead of time there was liable to be a fog coming in," he remembers. "Syd Halter kept pushing and pushing and telling me to run the game pretty fast. 'Keep it going, keep it going. We're liable to get a fog.' Sure enough, by the fourth quarter we were having difficulty." The fog prevented the fans in attendance from witnessing brilliant performances by Ticat Garney Henley and Blue Bomber Leo Lewis, who scored two touchdowns, threw for another, rushed 41 yards, and caught seven passes for 77 yards.

Henley was even better. The great two-way performer from South Dakota is fifth all-time with 59 interceptions; he also caught passes through each of his 16 seasons, a record that still stands. He was an All-Canadian defensive back nine straight seasons, 1963-1971. Considered one of the greatest defensive players of all time, in 1972 he made the All-Canadian offensive team as a receiver and won the Schenley award for Most Outstanding Player. Three years after he hung up his cleats, he was inducted into the Canadian Football Hall of Fame. No one has been elevated to that select company sooner upon retiring.

During the 1962 Grey Cup, Henley tallied two majors, 100 yards rushing and 119 yards on five pass receptions, as well as 47 yards on returns, the second-best total in a Grey Cup game.

Early in the fourth quarter, Don Sutherin picked up a single on a missed field goal attempt. The Bombers led by one. By this time, the fog was so low, Dojack wouldn't see the down markers from the far hash marks. The two GMs and Syd Halter huddled in consultation. In an unprecedented move, Commissioner Halter called the game with 9:29 remaining. Play would resume the following day with third down Hamilton at the Winnipeg 40 yard line.

Hamilton's great defensive lineman, John Barrow, didn't think their chance to move the ball in amounted to much. "Instead of having a coin toss and a kickoff the next day, which would have been fair, we began on third down, which meant Winnipeg would have immediate possession. Winnipeg had all night to think about what they were going to do the next day," he said.

Kenny Ploen remembered the difficulty of coming back the next day. "It was a most unusual thing in my mind — I guess only a football player can appreciate this — of playing the way we did on Saturday and then having to come back the next morning and have a pre-game meal, strap up, and go out and play that last nine minutes or so. You're so damn stiff. I'm sure it took everybody on both sides quite a while to get going. I know there were a couple of our players that didn't even go out onto the field. They tried, but they were black and blue and they just couldn't play."

The Ticats went right to their hotel rooms, but Bomber coach, Bud Grant, approached things differently. "Use your head," he said to the team. "Go on out, see what's going on out there. You know you've got to play tomorrow." Grant's use of psychology worked. The players went out for a little while, but were in bed pretty early, setting themselves a curfew of 11 p.m.

Most of the Ticats caught a movie and hit the sack, but Angelo Mosca, the most colourful Cat of them all, longed for some action on a Saturday night. "Bob Minihane and I said, 'Shucks, we can play nine minutes standing on our heads.' We went downtown and flagged a cab. There's got to be 10,000 taxis in Toronto, but we flag down one with our assistant coach Ralph Sazio in it!"

Joe Zuger was a rookie in 1962, participating in the first of 10 Grey Cups as a Ticat player or general manager. Like most of his teammates, he found the Fog Bowl the hardest Grey Cup to take. "I hurt my left ankle during the game. All I did the next day was punt. We were really on a high for the game. Then we had to come back the next day. We didn't get much sleep the night before the second day. We just went in with our equipment on, took it off, and went to bed, got up, and put it on again. It wasn't a good night."

When play resumed the next day, Joe Zuger couldn't continue at quarterback so Hamilton replaced him with second string quarterback Frank Cosentino. The Cats dominated the last nine minutes, but penalties and mistakes killed one scoring drive after another. Finally, Joe Zuger limped onto the field to try for a single that would send the two teams into overtime for the second straight year. It didn't even make it to the goal line. The final score was Winnipeg 28, Hamilton 27.

When analyzing the Fog Bowl, Angelo Mosca believed the damage had been done the previous day. "We should have won the Grey Cup," he said. "Don Sutherin missed two converts. We came back, ran all over them, and did everything except score a touchdown."

It is almost unheard of to miss a convert. Don Sutherin missed two. For the future Hall of Famer who still holds the record for most Grey Cup converts at 17, the Fog Bowl was a nightmare. Not only was it his third loss in three Grey Cups, but he felt personally responsible for the defeat. "There was a discrepancy over a field goal that I had kicked and I missed two extra points that day," Sutherin said. "As a matter of fact, it boiled down to where those were the points that cost us the ball game. You just don't miss extra points. I did, and that was the deciding factor in that Grey Cup. It was a very disappointing afternoon."

The MVP of the Fog Bowl was Bomber back Leo Lewis, one of the greatest players of all time. The six-time All-Star scored 79 touchdowns during his 12-year career and ranks sixth in rushing. His 776 combined yards is still the career Grey Cup record. Ironically, that was the only Grey Cup where the MVP didn't receive a truck or a car.

Winnipeg fell on hard times for the next two years, finishing out of the playoffs. In 1964, due to a horrendous string of injuries, they were 1-14-1. Hamilton, in the meantime, defeated B.C. 21-10 in Vancouver to win the 1963 Grey Cup.

The Lions turned the tables the following season 34-24 in Toronto. In 1965, the Blue Bombers returned to the big game against their old rivals. Mother Nature intervened again. In what came to be called the Wind Bowl, rather than punt into the gale, the Bombers conceded three safeties worth six points. Hamilton won 22-16.

Chapter 5
Grey Cup 1966:
Saskatchewan
vs. Ottawa

I f there is such a thing as Canada's team, it would be the Saskatchewan Roughriders. Formed in 1910, the Roughriders have survived two world wars, the Great Depression, 30 losing seasons, and the longest playoff drought in league history. They have won only two Grey Cups. The team mascot is Gainer the Gopher, but considering the team has had a "Save the Roughriders" fundraising campaign every few years, it should be a cat. This is an organization with at least nine lives.

Rider fans are known to be the best in the country. Despite 18 losing seasons between 1978 and 2002, the team drew an average of over 24,000 fans per game. During that period, the population of the province was showing only marginal growth, and the farm economy was almost as bad as in the Dirty Thirties. Roughrider support is even more remarkable considering Saskatchewan has the highest percentage of senior citizens in the country and Regina the largest percentage of First Nation Canadians, neither group known for their personal wealth.

Impressive as their home fan base may be, there are even more Rider fans living beyond the province's borders. The Jolly Green Giants play before a friendly sea of green and white in Calgary and Edmonton, and general managers of those teams have always tried to get the Roughriders scheduled late in the season. Rider fans will come out no matter what the circumstances or weather.

Their opponent for the 1966 national championship would be the Ottawa Rough Riders.

The Ottawa Football Club was formed at the Russell Hotel on September 18, 1876. They won their first Grey Cup as the Senators in 1925, defeating the Winnipeg Tammany Tigers 24-1. They repeated as champions in 1926 with a 10-7 win over the University of Toronto. Ottawa lost the 1936 Cup to Sarnia, those in 1939 and '41 to Winnipeg, to Calgary in '48, while beating Toronto Balmy Beach in 1940, Saskatchewan in 1951, and Edmonton in 1960.

The western team was born as the Regina Rugby Club at a December 1910 meeting in City Hall. Between 1911 and 1935 they finished first in the Western Rugby Union every year, playing in and losing seven Grey Cups. Their last appearance at the big dance during the first half of the 20th century was in 1934.

Grey Cup 1966: Saskatchewan vs. Ottawa

The historical jury is still out as to how both teams ended up with the same name. One account says there was a contingent of Canadian volunteers who fought with Teddy Roosevelt in the Spanish-American War. His troops were called the Roughriders with unit colours of red and black.

Some of those soldiers were with the Regina and Ottawa football teams and wanted the name. In 1924, the Ottawa Rough Riders changed their name to the Senators and Regina, heretofore called The Football Club, promptly called themselves the Roughriders. Three years later, Ottawa dropped Senators in favour of their old moniker.

Roosevelt's Roughriders is one word, not two, so it seems feasible that the Regina Roughriders were named after the heroes of the Spanish-American War, leaving the Rough Riders to be named after lumberjacks who rode logs down the Ottawa River.

The two franchises had more in common than their name. Until 1948, both teams wore black and red. That year the Westerners switched to green and white to take advantage of a bargain. Rider executive Jack Fyffe found two sets of green and white jerseys on sale in a Chicago store. Because the price was so low, Fyffe snapped them up and the green and white tradition was born.

In the second half of the last century, Saskatchewan appeared in eight Grey Cups, half against Ottawa, the first in 1951 when the Rough Riders defeated them 21-14.

With the arrival of Frank Clair as the head coach of

the Ottawa Rough Riders in 1956 and Ken Preston as the Saskatchewan general manager two years later, the two teams began to assemble power houses. During the '60s, Ottawa would play in four Grey Cups. Saskatchewan played three, and they'd play twice against each other. Their 1966 and '69 Cup battles featured two of the greatest teams in CFL history.

Ontario native Ken Preston knew the key to winning the Grey Cup was having quality Canadians. He inherited linemen Ron Atchison, Bill Clarke, and Reggie Whitehouse. He signed Ted Urness, who became the greatest centre to ever play the game. Talented receivers Gord Barwell and Al Ford came aboard along with defenders Wayne Shaw, Ted Dushinski, Larry Dumelie, Henry Dorsch, Dale West, and return man Gene Wlasiuk.

Americans added to the mix included receivers Hugh Campbell and Jim Worden, halfback Ed Buchanan, offensive linemen Al Benecik, Clyde Brock, Jack Abdenshan, and the soon-to-be legendary defensive lineman Ed McQuarters. The team was defined and forever remembered by the exploits of quarterback Ron Lancaster and fullback George Reed. The head coach was the Big Bird from Turkey Neck Bend, Kentucky, Eagle Keys. Ten members of the '66 team are in the Hall of Fame.

Ron Lancaster came into the league with Ottawa in 1958. But, when Canadian Russ Jackson arrived on the scene, the Little General was sent west to Saskatchewan in 1963. "I was traded to Saskatchewan for not very much," Lancaster recalled. "I think I went for the waiver price ($500). There were no players involved. I always said I went for a broken helmet with no face mask."

Until his records were eclipsed in 2004 by Damon Allen, Lancaster was the CFL's all-time leading passer. His friendly disposition masked an intense competitive spirit, evident not only as a player, but also as a future coach of Edmonton and Hamilton. The darling of football fans in Saskatchewan, he was nonetheless booed during his final appearance at Taylor Field in 1978. The little Pennsylvanian has been one of the great individuals in the Canadian game.

Just as fierce in his determination to win was George Reed, the CFL's all-time leading rusher until 2004. He still holds the record for rushing touchdowns with 134, as well as a dozen playoff and Grey Cup records. Although deeply admired by Saskatchewan fans, he caused considerable resentment when he said Regina was worse than Alabama when it came to racism. A proud man, Reed refused to play the Uncle Tom role by going along to get along. Both Reed's and Lancaster's career records have stood into the 21st century.

Assistant coach Jack Gotta described the 1966 Roughriders. "Football is a great team sport. Those guys had that. Black, white, young, old, Canadian, American, everybody got along. We had some bright people on that club. Ronnie Lancaster was a student of the game. I don't think George Reed ever blew an assignment. Everybody took such pride in what they were doing."

As the 1966 season began, the Roughriders' challenge was to accomplish what no other Saskatchewan team had done before: win the Grey Cup. Like Ottawa, Saskatchewan had topped their division for the first time since 1951. They won the best of three Western Finals in two games over Winnipeg when, trailing late in the game 19-14, Ed McQuarters scooped up a fumble and ran for the winning touchdown. Ottawa won the Eastern two-game total point final 72-17. The Grey Cup would be played in Vancouver on November 26. Ottawa was so heavily favoured that the television networks set up their cameras in the Eastern dressing room early in the third quarter to get post-game comment.

Dale West: "The television cameras were in the Ottawa Rough Rider dressing room, so if anybody wanted to get interviewed, they had to walk across to the Ottawa side."

Said Eagle Keys, "We never should have been six-point underdogs. But the publicity sure didn't hurt. The way folks were writing about the game, you'd have thought we didn't belong on the same field as Ottawa. That got to our fellows a bit. They have pride in themselves and they didn't enjoy being downgraded so much. We had beaten some pretty good teams to get there."

Only two Roughriders had any Grey Cup experience, the quarterback and the coach. Eagle Keys readied his troops for the big game. "Unless you're prepared to dedicate yourself to the Grey Cup game, you don't deserve to win it," he said. "If you don't prepare and discipline yourself, you'll lose it because of mistakes. And you don't want to make mistakes and lose it because you went down there to have a good time."

While Ottawa whooped it up in downtown Vancouver, Keys had his team secluded in nearby Burnaby. A good thing too, because at the Grey Cup parade on the Friday night before the game, a riot broke out. It took 150 police and the K-9 corps to restore order. About 689 people were arrested.

"Eagle had us out of town," remembered Ed McQuarters. "We were totally focused because everybody was expecting big things from us. We were isolated."

Roughrider strategy against Ottawa was simple: run, run, run, and run some more, not only to advance the ball and score, but also to eat up the clock. Ottawa liked to go with a spread line by splitting defenders outside, giving Reed and Buchanan the opportunity to find gaps and capitalize on blocking angles. Despite the offence of Russ Jackson, Whit Tucker, Bo Scott, Ron Stewart, Ted Watkins, Jay Roberts, and Jim Dillard, Keys felt the opposition's greatest strength was defence. And his ace in the hole would be Ron Lancaster.

When No. 23 came into the league from the American NFL, he had a reputation as a scrambling, running quarterback. Once the diminutive pivot learned the Canadian game, he became one of the greatest passers of all time. He was called the Little General because of his brilliance in directing his attack. At a time when quarterbacks didn't use checkoffs or audibles much (changing or calling the play at the line of scrimmage), Lancaster had mastered that art. Against Ottawa he would be audible 80 percent of the time, keeping the East's superb defence off-balance.

When it came time for player introductions at the big game, the Westerners were incredibly tense. A timely pratfall may very well have been the turning point in the greatest day in the history of Saskatchewan sports.

When the announcer called out No. 53, Jack Abendshan, the New Mexico-born star headed out of the tunnel at Empire Stadium. On his way out to the biggest game of his career, Abendshan slipped and fell on the muddy track. When he got up, amid peals of laughter, he had a big muddy patch on his rear end. It may have been embarrassing at the time, but that fall may have been just the right amount of comic relief.

Abendshan kicked off at 2 p.m. under an overcast sky, with a temperature of 8° C. Assisted by two Saskatchewan offsides, Russ Jackson marched Ottawa in five plays to their 49-yard line. Then Saskatchewan's Dale West saw Ottawa halfback Ron Stewart come through the line. Thinking it was a run, West came up to help out the linebackers. Ottawa receiver Whit Tucker blew by him, taking Jackson's 61-yard pass on the dead run to the end zone. Moe "The Toe" Racine missed the convert.

West soon atoned for his sin by intercepting at the Ottawa 43 when receiver Ted Watkins got tangled up with Saskatchewan defender Ted Dushinski and fell down. The ball came right to West who returned it to the nine-yard line.

On the second down of that possession, tight end Jim

Worden told Lancaster he could beat Ottawa's Gene Gaines. A master ball handler, Lancaster set up the pass by faking Reed into the line and finding Worden deep in the end zone.

"Jim Worden was telling Ronnie that he could beat Gene Gaines," Ford recalled. "After the touchdown Worden came back to the huddle and said, "I told you I could beat him deep." The convert was good. Gaines gave all the credit to the quarterback. "Ronnie Lancaster was a great actor. He stuck the ball in George's gut and then pulled it out, and the next thing you know Worden is wide open and bang, touchdown. We all took a bite out of it, we all took the bait."

The underdogs led after 15 minutes 7-6, even though Ottawa had 147 yards to Saskatchewan's 45. The green and white went offside five times in the first quarter, probably a record.

In the second quarter, linebacker Wally Dempsey snuffed out an Ottawa drive at his 33 by wrestling the ball away from Jay Roberts. Soon after, Lancaster threw toward Alan Ford in the end zone. At the last moment, Ottawa defensive back Bob O'Billovich stuck a hand up to deflect it away or make the interception. The ball went right through his hands. Ford caught the pass easily.

Saskatchewan 14, Ottawa 6.

On Ottawa's first play from scrimmage after returning the ball to the 25, Jackson was flushed out of the pocket. Running for his life, he rifled the ball down field to a streaking Whit Tucker who was being dogged by Dale West. Jackson

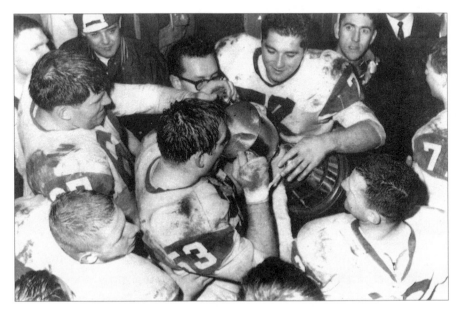

The Saskatchewan Roughriders celebrate their Grey Cup
victory over the Ottawa Rough Riders, Vancouver, 1966

lobbed the ball over his head, a mistake West wouldn't be allowed to forget for a long time. For several years, CTV opened their football telecasts with a shot of West chasing Tucker into the end zone.

Bill Kline added a single, making the score 14-all at half-time.

Just before the end of the scoreless third quarter, Kline punted from his end zone. Gene Wlasiuk returned it to the Ottawa 32-yard line. Five plays into the final quarter, Lancaster found Campbell in the end zone. The green were up by seven.

Ottawa went three-and-out on their ensuing possession. Starting at the Ottawa 47-yard line, Buchanan ran for six
and Reed for 10 to the 31. On the next play, he blazed his way
to the end zone. With the convert and a Ford single, the final
score was Saskatchewan 29, Ottawa 14. The longest Grey Cup
drought in CFL history was over.

The Roughies picked up 169 yards rushing in the second half. Defensively, they held the eastern Riders to one
first down in each of the second and third quarters and two
in the fourth near the end of the game. George Reed talked
about what happened. "We never got away from our ground
game," he said. "We were able to keep pounding away.
Lancaster threw a couple of passes that put us in a position
to deliver the knock-out punch. I happened to be the knock-
out punch."

For Ron Atchison, it was never in doubt. "In a lot of
Grey Cups, the game is won one way or another before you
ever get on the field. We were down early in the first quarter,
but we never even thought of losing. We were beating them
on the line. We were just up better for that game. We were
six-point underdogs, but we had a real good feeling. It's an
inner feeling. I noticed it lots of times. Lots of times, four or
five minutes into the game, I could tell you whether we were
going to win or lose. By the time you get to the Grey Cup, the
teams are pretty evenly matched. You've got good men every-
where. So it's a matter of who is really going to take charge."

Three years later, they would meet again.

Chapter 6
Grey Cup 1969: Ottawa vs. Saskatchewan

For the Ottawa Rough Riders, the '60s were their golden age. Thirteen members of those ball clubs are enshrined in the Canadian Football Hall of Fame. They appeared in four Grey Cups, winning three. They were led by that rarest of individuals in the modern era of football, a Canadian quarterback.

Russ Jackson wasn't drafted as a quarterback. Taken as a defensive back in 1958, it was only injuries to Hal Ledyard and Tom Dimitroff that gave Jackson a shot late in the same year. His first contract was for $4700, with a $500 signing bonus and a ticket back and forth to Toronto to go to school. Jackson attended the Ontario College of Education in Toronto and only played for Ottawa on the weekends.

Grey Cup 1969: Ottawa vs. Saskatchewan

American coaches generally had little respect for Canadian players, especially quarterbacks. In fact, when Frank Clair coached Toronto (1950-54), the immortal Canadian star Joe Krol complained bitterly about Clair's lack of enthusiasm for homebrews. When Clair was forced to use Jackson, he reluctantly changed his tune. "Russ Jackson and Ronnie Stewart were stand-outs," he allowed. "Although they were Canadians, those two alone were the kingpins of our club."

"I never had the feeling that Clair didn't think I could do the job," said Jackson. "It took some time to earn the full confidence of everybody, but I think that's true for any quarterback. I was in the right place at the right time, sure. That's true with any sport. You can be in the wrong place at the wrong time and never get the opportunity."

Clair and Jackson developed a close relationship, a key to their success. "Over the years, we started to think alike because I understood what he was trying to do. Near the end of my career, he very seldom sent any plays in. Often, Frank would say, 'The play you ran was the one I was thinking about.' When you spend that much time together, you begin to think alike and understand what you are trying to do during a football game."

During his career, Jackson completed 1356 of 2530 passes for 24,592 yards, 185 touchdowns, and 125 interceptions. He held the passing efficiency record for 14 years. His rushing total of 5045 yards is fourth-best all-time for a quarterback. Jackson won the Schenley Awards for Most Outstanding

Canadian four times, and Outstanding Player three times. He carried away both trophies in 1963, 1966, and 1969. A six-time All-Star, he was inducted into the Hall of Fame on May 16, 1973.

His sidekick in success during those years was another Canadian, halfback Ronnie Stewart, also joining the Rough Riders in 1958. Canada's Male Athlete of the Year in 1960, at 5 feet 7 inches and 180 pounds, Stewart overcame his small stature to become one of the greatest players in CFL history. He won three Cups, the Schenley Outstanding Canadian Player Award, and three All-Star selections. He, too, is in the Hall of Fame. In Montreal, on October 10, 1960, Stewart set the still-standing CFL single game rushing record of 287 yards, doing so on only 15 carries.

Ottawa began their golden decade by winning the Grey Cup, defeating the Eagle Keys Edmonton Eskimos 16-6. Between 1961 and '65, Ottawa was always the bridesmaid, with five straight second-place finishes. "We had a lot of good teams," said Jackson. "But we could never beat Hamilton or cross that threshold to get to the Grey Cup. It was discouraging in the early '60s. Then in the late '60s we became the dominant team. We were unbeatable at home and went to the Grey Cup three times."

They lost the Cup to Saskatchewan in 1966. Two years later they beat Calgary 24- 21, setting the stage for a rematch with the Western Riders on a frozen field at Montreal's Autostade on November 30, 1969. It was an opportunity for

Jackson, Stewart, and Frank Clair to avenge their only Grey Cup defeat, after which they would retire.

"It was a very emotional time for me, personally," Jackson said. "I'd announced at the start of the season it was going to be my last year. After we got to the Grey Cup and I won the Schenley Award again, I know the pressure was on everybody to make it a fairy-tale ending."

During the early going, it looked like Jackson's dream of going out on a winning note would turn into a nightmare. Ed McQuarters and the man they called the Undertaker, Bill Baker, were planning an early retirement party for their arch rival.

Said McQuarters, "Russ Jackson was very mobile, very tough, a very strong physical type.

"Bill Baker and I were actually sitting in the dressing room before the game trying to figure a way to get to Jackson. He had this one bar on his helmet that hung down to almost under his chin. So here's Baker saying, 'Well, if I hit him this way by throwing an elbow, I can get in there and break his nose and get him out of the game.' So here we are plotting how we were going to get Russ Jackson out of the game. It never happened. He was too tough for that."

Unbeknownst to the fans and football personnel, the Grey Cup game was played under the pall of a terrorist threat. The FLQ (Front du Libération du Québec) planned to disrupt the proceedings and possibly try to assassinate Prime Minister Pierre Elliott Trudeau, who would be in attendance.

Responsibility for staging the game rested with the commissioner Jake Gaudaur.

"The game was in Montreal at the peak of the FLQ problem," he explained. "There were threats that the FLQ was going to stage a march and walk toward the Grey Cup parade. Day after day, he debated pulling the game out of Montreal.

Finally, two weeks before the game, the word came from Ottawa that a decision had been made. The Grey Cup was not going to be disrupted, because the terrorists thought it would be counterproductive to their cause. So, Gaudaur gambled and went ahead with the game in Montreal. But he was prepared. All around the stadium, in every light standard, there were both cameras and sharpshooters.

"As a final condition of staging the game in Montreal, I demanded assurances from Mayor Jean Drapeau that there would be adequate policing on the site," Gaudaur said. "With three minutes to go, I'm looking down on the field, and all of a sudden, I see all these police in riot gear coming out of the entrance. There were enough of them to ring the field shoulder to shoulder. They made a decision to overprotect."

Despite the protection, some damage was done: the trophy was stolen after the game. "What I did along the way, was take the original Grey Cup and put it safely in the Hall of Fame," said Gaudaur. "I had a replica produced. I did that after it was stolen and recovered by the Ottawa police early in 1970. At that time, I decided we shouldn't lose the symbol of what we were supposed to be all about and decided to protect it in that way."

On the field, though, a different war was being waged. Saskatchewan took a 9-0 lead in the first quarter on a 27-yard Ron Lancaster pass to Alan Ford and a safety touch conceded by Billy Van Burkleo. Then, Jackson and Stewart began one of the most amazing performances in Grey Cup history.

Jackson marched his team almost the length of the field before completing a 12-yard pass to Jay Roberts for a touchdown. Soon after, Jackson tossed a short one to Ronnie Stewart, who went 80 yards for the score, giving the Red Riders a 14-9 half-time lead.

The third touchdown came when Jackson eluded a ferocious pass rush at the Saskatchewan 12-yard line and found Jim Mankins alone in the end zone. He admitted it was a broken play.

"We were rolling right and [Ed] McQuarters had me right in his grasp and I happened to get lucky and get away from him. I came back across the grain and Mankins was standing there just over the goal line and there it was."

Ottawa's last major came in similar fashion. This time Saskatchewan's Cliff Shaw had Jackson in his grasp, but somehow he got the ball to Stewart who ran 32 yards for the score. Given Jackson's prowess as a deep passer, defences tended to ignore his short game. Jackson and Stewart picked up Saskatchewan's all-out blitz. Stewart let it through and then drifted into the flat where Jackson hit him on the run. He went the distance for the touchdown.

"Things went well. We happened to read the Saskatchewan blitzes well and scored a couple of long touchdown passes with Ronnie Stewart — not on two long passes, but long runs. These things happen when you are prepared, and we did the job that particular day. If you ask people to whom we threw four touchdown passes in 1969, they'd probably mention Atkins, Washington, Tucker, but it turned out to be Jay Roberts, Jim Mankins, and Ronnie Stewart. None of the big wheels had touchdown catches."

Later, Ford and Jack Abendshan added singles in quarter number three, but that's all she wrote. The day belonged to Ottawa. The final score was Ottawa 29, Saskatchewan 11.

Like Eagle Keys, Frank Clair stressed preparation. "The players were very aware that I meant business about preparing myself. We worked very hard and we were very precise in what we did. We tried to eliminate every mistake we could make and be in complete readiness. The players sensed this from our coaching staff. You've got to have players believing that the coaches are doing everything to win and that they can win. You want the players to feel that this is the most important thing in their whole life."

Jackson's four touchdown passes set a still unmatched Grey Cup record. Alan Ford starred for Saskatchewan with a touchdown, single, and a record 78-yard kickoff return.

Jackson explained what turned the also-rans into winners. "We never went into a ball game in the last half of the '60s thinking we could lose. You go with that feeling you know you're going to find a way to win rather than find a way to lose."

Ron Lancaster said, "That was one of those days where it went almost the way it was written, that Russ was going to retire and he was going to win. Stewart had a great game. We didn't play the Ottawa game in '69 like we played Ottawa in '66. In '66, the longer the game went, the more we got control of it. In '69, they got control and dominated late in the game. That's why they won."

You didn't have to convince Saskatchewan coach Eagle Keys that Jackson and Stewart were destiny's darlings. "There are some games you get the feeling you're not going to be allowed to win," he drawled. "That was one of them."

Jackson looked back at his Grey Cup career. "The first one in 1960 was kind of neat because we were all young Canadian kids, not just me but a lot of us — Gary Schreider, Lou Bruce, Ted Smale, Ronnie Stewart. You dream of winning a Grey Cup when you're a kid in Canada. That one was special. For me, personally, 1969 was just as big."

Many think Jackson was the best ever. "It is nice to be considered in the top group," he said quietly. "I don't think anybody can pick the best. We all played in different eras, the games were different, whether it's football, hockey or baseball. If you're considered and your name comes up when you're talking about the best, you figure it must have been a pretty good time."

Chapter 7
Grey Cup 1981:
Edmonton
vs. Ottawa

The greatest dynasty in Canadian football history was the Edmonton Eskimos. The Alberta team won an unprecedented five straight Grey Cups between 1978 and 1982. As a prelude to that remarkable run, they went to the big game four times in five years (1973-77), winning in 1975. After missing a year, they returned to the infamous Staple Bowl at Montreal's Olympic Stadium in 1977, losing to Les Alouettes 41-6 on a surface more suitable for hockey. Between 1973 and 1982, Edmonton made it to the Grey Cup nine out of ten years, winning six times. The only team in professional sport to do better was the basketball Boston Celtics of the '50s and '60s.

The genius of the Eskimos has been finding the right

man at the right time and sticking with a grand design. The club has been a shrewd judge of personnel, often thinking outside the box. When they make a mistake, they admit it quickly and move on.

The key to success for any professional team is the general manager. The man who put the dynasty together in Edmonton was Norm Kimball, inducted into the CFL Hall of Fame in 1991. Before joining the Eskimos in 1961 as coordinator of minor football, Kimball spent nine years working for the National Cash Register Company and coaching minor football. There was little in his background that would indicate he would be one of the best managers in football history, on either side of the border. Kimball made a lot of changes in an organization that struggled after its success in the 1950s. He built on what he knew, developing local talent, and when it came to that, he was a visionary. He started by hosting camps to scout out talented kids on their way to college. Kimball and his staff fed the information to universities, mostly in the northwestern U.S. and essentially set up a perpetual talent machine. Eventually, the colleges started coming to Kimball.

Other teams in the Western Conference envied Edmonton's success, attributing it to unlimited resources, but Kimball's shrewd planning, not money, was a key factor in building the dynasty. Edmonton had no more money than the other teams. The trick was where to spend it. "We spent more money on scouting than other teams," he said. "We stayed in the best places, we travelled the best way, we did everything to make it better for the player, and then we asked for a lot of him in return."

Norm Kimball hired the best scouts in the business, Ray Neuman and Frankie Morris. "Ray did a great job," Kimball recalled. "We always had people coming in, especially at quarterback. We were never in the position that if somebody went down, we couldn't replace him. Frank Morris had a great ability to deal with young people. I saw that when he was working at the University of Alberta. He was absolutely outstanding in dealing with our Canadian prospects and in college scouting."

Morris was a lineman on the Argo team that won three consecutive Grey Cups, 1945-47 and the Eskimos that took three straight, 1954-56. He described his art. "You have to know people, who to talk to. I did some things that I think were a little different. I got to know a whole lot of trainers and equipment people. They enjoy talking to you. I got a lot of good information from them. If you want to really know a kid's character, ask the trainer or equipment man."

What gave Edmonton the edge? Morris knew what he was looking for. "I've told this story many times over about our Argonaut club of 1947 and the great Eskimo teams of the '50s, '70s, and '80s. I've always said the parts were interchangeable. Same type of individuals: a bunch of guys who liked to play hard. They liked one another, they got along real well, they had a whole lot of pride, and were a heck of a pile of good athletes. I was lucky to be associated with three groups of guys like that. It was marvellous.

"There was an atmosphere. It's funny. When I'd go visit NFL clubs, I could walk on to their training site and, honest to God, when I walked in the door, I almost knew immediately whether it was a winning or losing situation — just the atmosphere around those places. That's what the Eskimos had. People would come in and feel like winners. I don't know how you define that, but I really think it was true."

As late as 2004, you could find Frankie Morris, Jackie Parker, and other former Eskimo greats in the press box at Commonwealth Stadium. Stability, continuity, honouring the past, building for the future — these were the hallmarks of Edmonton Eskimo success.

After getting to the Grey Cup in 1960, the Eskimos didn't win a single playoff game for the rest of the decade. When they finished out of the money in 1969, Kimball fired head coach Neil Armstrong. He ignored the obvious choices of more experienced individuals, and replaced him with assistant Ray Jauch, who at 32 became the youngest head coach in the CFL.

Jauch graduated from Iowa in 1960 and joined the Winnipeg Blue Bombers. His playing career ended abruptly during the 1961 Grey Cup when he blew his Achilles tendon, the only player in Cup history to do so. In 1966, Neil Armstrong hired him as an assistant. Kimball explained why he promoted him. "I thought he was very competitive, a bright young guy. He wanted to win so badly that I knew he would work hard to get it done."

In Jauch's rookie season in 1970, the Eskimos finished second and he won the Coach of the Year Award. He wasn't satisfied, though, and was particularly upset with the attitude of some of his players before the team's semi-final loss to Calgary. Although they had made the playoffs, the guys had their cars packed and in the parking lot, ready to go home. Jauch thought that was garbage. He wanted them to be accountable to the community. He wanted them to have to walk down the street the next day, figuring it was a matter of attitude, of playing harder, of having to face the fans rather than get out of town.

Although they made post-season play, Jauch knew that a lot of changes had to be made if the club was to win a Grey Cup. He got rid of a lot of veterans and stuck with his fresh faces through thick and thin. The result? Jauch went from hero to bum in a matter of months, with the Eskimos finishing last in 1971. But they haven't missed the playoffs since. Jauch's journey to the top of the Western Conference began in a strange way.

The Eskimos had really struggled against the dominant team in the league, the Saskatchewan Roughriders. Like most football teams, the Eskimos played basketball during the off-season to raise money for charity and to stay in shape. When the Roughriders came to play a charity game at the University of Alberta, Jauch said, "Listen, I don't give a damn, we're going to beat these guys at something. I don't care what it is — checkers or whatever — but we're going to beat those guys and, by golly, let's go out and beat them at basketball. Let's get this thing started." They won the basketball game, and from then on the team had a winning attitude.

Jauch began to assemble the dynasty with retreads and rejects. He signed B.C. cast-offs defensive end Ron Estay, centre Bob Howse, and quarterback Tom Wilkinson. During Wilkinson's 15-year CFL career, the 5 feet 9 inches, 177 pound quarterback from Wyoming completed 1613 of 2662 passes for 22,579 yards and 154 touchdowns. He holds the record for highest pass completion percentage in a single game at 90.5 percent. Three times he was the All-Canadian quarterback. He won the Most Outstanding Player award in 1974 and entered the CFL Hall of Fame in 1987. He has five Grey Cup rings.

Wilkie began his CFL career with Toronto in 1967. In 1971, Argo coach Leo Cahill shipped Wilkinson to B.C. because Argo owner John Bassett didn't believe Wilkie looked like a quarterback. When he was cut by the Lions, he called Jauch and said he was thinking of driving home to Grey Bull, Wyoming, but wanted to know if Edmonton might have room for a back-up quarterback. Jauch invited him on board. He still lives in Edmonton.

Jauch didn't know what he was getting in Wilkinson. "I really didn't, not until I walked into the locker room with him and I could see the reaction of the players. He brought a desire, a willingness to put himself secondary to everything else. The players loved to play with him."

Said Hugh Campbell, "Wilkinson was our number one leader. He had great athletic ability that was camouflaged with his build, being short and squatty. But he was a competitor at the highest level. He was the single best leader I've ever been around as far as team play goes."

The great linebacker Dan Kepley recalled coming into the dressing room on his first day in Edmonton. He had just arrived from the NFL Dallas Cowboys' camp, where he played with the great Roger Staubach. Kepley ran into a little fat guy, chewing tobacco and holding a sluice cup in his hand. Wilkinson stuck out his free hand to greet the new arrival and told him he was the quarterback. Kepley snorted with derision, figuring the little guy was the equipment manager or trainer.

Kepley soon learned looks can be deceiving.

"He was a man that absolutely got the best and most out of what he had and he would find a way to get it done. He wasn't pretty, but he was effective. He was the best all-round athlete I have ever seen in my life. The best. He was drafted by major league baseball. He can shoot the eyes out of a basketball. He shoots pool, he bowls, he knows every card game, he's a ping-pong player, he golfs. He was an A squash and racquetball player. He is the most intelligent athlete I have ever met."

Another key element in Eskimo success was place

kicker Dave Cutler. Jauch didn't really know what he was getting with him, either. In fact, Cutler's career was almost over before it began.

After struggling through his rookie year, he started to show improvement in 1970, Jauch's first year as head coach. But then he missed a convert in Vancouver and a few plays later a field goal was blocked because of his low trajectory. At that point, a disgruntled Jauch called on Peter Kempf to go in and kick. Cutler watched Kempf search frantically for his place-kicking shoe. Cutler ran by him on to the field and kicked one in from the 43-yard line. He was back on track and on his way to a future date with the Hall of Fame.

When Jauch was reminded that he almost benched one of the greatest place kickers in CFL history, he laughed, "We always weren't so smart, were we? Thank God Kempf couldn't find his shoe."

After retooling his line-up with competitors like Wilkinson, the Eskimos were ready to roll. In 1972, they went from last to a first place tie with Winnipeg. They lost the semi-final 8-6 to the Roughriders. The next three years they finished first, losing the Grey Cup to Ottawa in 1973 and Montreal in '74, and beating the Alouettes in '75. In '76, they fell back to third. Jauch was promoted to director of football operations. In another stroke of personnel genius, Kimball and Jauch hired former Saskatchewan great Hugh Campbell out of tiny Whitworth College in Spokane, Washington.

At age 36, Campbell was the youngest, least experienced

coach in the CFL. He hired veteran assistants Leo McKillip and Joe Faragalli, adding Cal Murphy the following year. He also hired a young man who had no coaching experience beyond the high school level, except for a graduate assistant-ship at the University of Idaho. His name was Don Matthews, now the winningest coach in CFL history.

The *Edmonton Journal* heaped its disapproval on the new coach's head with the headline "Campbell Hires High School Coach." But Campbell knew Matthews was special. The following year, he made him his defensive coordinator.

With the coaching staff intact, the greatest run in league history was about to begin. The Eskimos finished in a three-way tie for first, and trounced B.C. in the Western Final, before being annihilated 41-6 by Montreal in the Grey Cup. The following year, quarterback Warren Moon joined the team along with receivers Tommy Scott and Bryan Fryer, as well as Hec Pothier, who allowed Campbell to go with an offensive line comprising only Canadians. They made it back to the Grey Cup, defeating the Als 20-13. In 1979, starry receiver Brian Kelly arrived. Montreal and Edmonton clashed again in 1979, with the Eskimos winning a tough defensive struggle 17-9.

The Eskimos rolled to their third straight Grey Cup championship by taming the Ticats 48-10 in 1980. That set up an 1981 opportunity to win an unprecedented fourth Grey Cup in a row.

Many believe the 1981 edition of the Eskimos, who went

Grey Cup 1981: Edmonton vs. Ottawa

14-1-1, were the greatest team in CFL history. Warren Moon and Tom Wilkinson combined to set a new passing record. Dave Cutler established five career marks and the Esks set a record of most points scored in a season with 576. They averaged 36 points a game while giving up only 17. They beat B.C. to advance to the Grey Cup against an Ottawa team that had only won five games. It looked like a mismatch of gigantic proportions.

A victory for the Capitol Hill gang was unthinkable, and it would have been the greatest upset in the history of Canadian sports. But what should have been a hopeless situation turned out to be one of the most glorious days in the history of the Ottawa franchise. But how does a coach prepare a team facing a hopeless situation?

"We had actually played pretty well against Edmonton during the season," said Rider boss George Brancato. "Toward the end of the season, we started to get hot. Our quarterback, J.C. Watts, started to shake his injuries and play well. We were really loose the week before. Nobody expected us to win. I don't think the game was even on the boards for betting because everybody was sure Edmonton was going to win."

One of Ottawa's stars was Greg Marshall, who would be named the league's best defensive player in 1983. "We were actually pretty confident about our chances," he said. "We knew we could play with them. We didn't have anything to lose, nobody expected us to win, so we were just going to go out and play hard and see what happened. We knew that it would be hard not to be a little bit overconfident if you were Edmonton. If we could get something going early, we thought we'd have a chance."

In the first quarter, Ottawa's Gerry Organ made field goals of 34 and 37 yards. A minute and a half later, Jim Reid converted a turnover into a touchdown.

Led by the inspired play of Julius Caesar Watts, the Rough Riders enjoyed a 13-0 lead at the end of the first quarter.

Early in the second quarter, Sam Platt ran 14 yards for a major. All the mighty Eskimos could muster in the opening half was a single on a missed Dave Cutler field goal.

Just before the end of the half, Campbell pulled future NFL star Warren Moon and sent in the forgotten Tom Wilkinson. Wilkie strung together a few first downs and brought the sputtering offence to life, giving them some sense of optimism when they headed for the dressing room down 20-1.

At the half, Brancato told his players to keep doing what they were doing. The Riders stormed out of the locker room, and on Edmonton's first possession of the second half, intercepted Warren Moon and kicked a field goal, making the score 23-1 in favour of the 22-point underdog Ottawa Rough Riders. Then Edmonton woke up.

Trailing 23-1, Dan Kepley and Dave Fennell made crushing tackles and stopped the Riders cold. Then Jim Germany ran for a touchdown. After the defence held again, Moon came in to drive his team to the goal line, where he scored on a quarterback sneak.

Gerry Organ gave Ottawa an eight-point lead halfway through the final frame. But Moon scored again, and with the two-point convert, the game was tied.

Near the end, J.C. Watts threw to Tony Gabriel at the 55, but it was called double interference.

Brancato was incensed and with good reason. Gabriel had come back to the ball with Eskimo defensive back Gary Hayes draped all over him. Even then, he still made the catch, which could have been critical to the outcome, giving the Riders a first down at mid-field with an opportunity to move in for the winning field goal. Instead, the ball was back deep in Ottawa's end and, after Watts was sacked, Ottawa was forced to punt. Edmonton got the ball back in good field position.

Staring around mid-field, Moon quickly marched the Eskimos to the enemy 20. Dave Cutler kicked the winning field goal with three seconds left on the clock. Edmonton had won their fourth straight Cup 26-23. It was the greatest comeback in Grey cup history.

"I couldn't have drawn that game up better," commented Campbell. "I wouldn't have felt satisfied blowing Ottawa away like we did to Hamilton the year before. And to be able to win it on the last play! I preferred to win it by making a field goal rather than them missing one."

Almost pulling off the biggest upset in Canadian sports

history was something Ottawa could feel good about. "I suppose," said a doubtful Brancato. "But a loss is a loss. It's hard to take, especially a Grey Cup game. It hurt."

That was Ottawa's last hurrah. They never had another winning season. The franchise folded after the 1996 season only to be reborn six years later as the Renegades. Tom Wilkinson retired. Hugh Campbell's Eskimos made it five Grey Cups in a row by beating Toronto 32-16 the following year.

Chapter 8
Grey Cup 1989:
Saskatchewan
vs. Hamilton

*"Joseph said to Pharaoh: 'God has thus foretold to
Pharaoh what he is about to do. Seven years of great
abundance ... will be followed by seven years of famine ...
when all the abundance in the land ... will be forgotten.'"*
Genesis Chapter 41: 25-30.

oseph was a piker. Try 11 years of feast
and famine. Children grew into adults won-
dering why their beloved Saskatchewan
Roughriders were never allowed to win. Grey Cup? Finding
the Holy Grail would have been easier.

First the feast. From 1966 through 1976, the Roughriders
won more games than any team in the country. They appeared

in five Grey Cups, winning one. They garnered 48 All-Canadian selections, three Outstanding Player Awards, and one Coach of the Year Award. They appeared in the Western final in each of those 11 years. Eleven Riders from that era are in the CFL Hall of Fame.

And then a curse settled upon the land.

After one of the most incredible periods of success in Canadian football history, the Riders authored a new, likely never-to-be-broken record of futility, missing the playoffs 11 years in a row. Even the Great Depression only lasted 10 years.

After losing the 1976 Grey Cup to Ottawa in the last minute of play, the Riders finished 8-8 and fourth in 1977. They won a total of eight games between '78 and '80 before the exciting quarterback combination of John Hufnagel and Joe Barnes — dubbed J.J. Barnagel — led to a winning record in 1981. Their playoff hopes went down the drain on a rain-soaked field at B.C.'s Empire Stadium in the last game of that season. Back to the wilderness for six years. Then, in 1988, John Gregory, in his second year as head coach, brought them home in second place with a mark of 11-7. But they lost the semi-final to B.C. 42-18.

Saskatchewan began the 1989 campaign with a record of 4-1. Kent Austin and Tom Burgess gave the Riders their best quarterbacking since the days of Ron Lancaster. The Riders were explosive and exciting, scoring 547 points. But they only finished third. They closed out the regular season

The Saskatchewan Roughriders in 1989

by losing to Edmonton 49-17. A quick exit from the post-season seemed guaranteed.

Au contraire. Beginning the most magical period of Roughrider history, they went into Calgary and knocked off the Stampeders 33-26. The key play came on a second-and-long at the Calgary 46. Austin called a draw with little-used Canadian fullback Brian Walling, who ran it in for the winning touchdown.

Up to Edmonton, where the Eskimos had set a record by finishing first with a mark of 16-2. But one of those defeats was at the hands of the Roughriders. Although the home team was well-rested and ready, the underdog Roughriders won 32-21. The green and white headed for Toronto to meet

Hamilton at the Grey Cup christening of the eighth wonder of the world, SkyDome.

Saskatchewan had led the league in passing yardage and TD passes. The Ticats had been second in passing yardage and completions. Everything pointed to a shootout of epic proportions.

While there was no question Mike Kerrigan would start at quarterback for Hamilton, there was quarterback controversy in Regina. Would it be Tom Burgess or Kent Austin? John Gregory tended to play Tommy Burgess against blitzing teams (ones that rush the quarterback with as many as eight or nine players on almost all passing downs) and Kent Austin against a zone team (where the defenders hang back and pick up receivers who come into their area or zone). Hamilton was a zone team. He went with Austin. Fans were up in arms.

Rider assistant coach, Dick Adams, had a good feeling the night before the Grey Cup. It was a premonition, a dream. In his mind, he played the game and saw what the outcome was going to be. He saw a close game and he saw the Riders win it with a field goal at the end.

How he could have predicted this no one knows, but John Gregory had the same feeling.

Despite their confidence, the early going wasn't promising. On their second possession, Hamilton moved to the Rider 35 and kicked a field goal. Four plays later, a Frank Robinson interception set up a second field goal. After Saskatchewan replied with a single, Kerrigan capped off a 75-yard drive with a touchdown pass to Tony Champion. Hamilton led 13-1 at the end of the first quarter.

The fun began on their second possession of the quarter. Starting at his 48, Austin hit Jeff Fairholm for 22 yards. Austin missed on a long bomb to the end zone before connecting with Ray Elgaard for 16. Three plays later, he threw a five-yard strike to Elgaard for a touchdown. Hamilton 13, Saskatchewan 8.

Elgaard's 16-yard catch in the enemy 24 was a turning point. The Riders needed a big play to get them back in the game. The pass was in front of him, and he had to dive forward and grab it with one hand. Not only did the catch set up the ensuing touchdown grab, it gave the offence a tremendous and badly needed lift. After that, the Saskatchewan offence was just playing pitch and catch.

So was Hamilton. After taking the kickoff to their 53, Kerrigan picked up a first down to Estell. He threw to Rocky DiPietro at the 30 and to McAdoo for the touchdown. Hamilton 20, Saskatchewan 8. The Westerners were not fazed.

Then came the signature play of the 1989 Grey Cup.

It was first down at the Rider 35. Kent Austin came up behind centre Mike Anderson, whose father Paul had toiled for the green and white over 30 years before. Receiver Jeff Fairholm came up to the line, glancing over to his quarterback and thinking about his dad, Larry, in the SkyDome crowd that day, an Alouette veteran of the 1970 championship game. Austin dropped back to pass, looked to his right, glanced into the middle, and then found Fairholm streaking down the left side. At the moment he caught the ball, a flag came down, but the second-year slot broke through the interference and raced 75 yards for the touchdown.

The catch was the biggest of his professional career. "It will always be in my memory, there is no doubt about that. Every day I look at that football I caught," he said.

Hamilton was not impressed. With two strikes of 9 and 15 yards to Champion, 5 runs for 37 yards by McAdoo and an 11-yard completion to DiPietro, Kerrigan marched his team 71 yards for a major. Hamilton 27, Saskatchewan 15.

Again, Saskatchewan answered back. Three passes to James Ellingson, plus strikes to Narcisse and Elgaard brought them to the 5-yard line, where Austin found Narcisse alone in the end zone. At half-time, the scoreboard read Hamilton 27, Saskatchewan 22.

Saskatchewan had launched an all-out aerial attack. Austin was 11 for 16 and had three touchdowns in the second quarter. He went exclusively to the air, because when they ran the ball, Hamilton kept scoring. "We didn't run the ball one time in the second quarter," said Kent Austin.

"We couldn't afford to. We had to keep scoring to keep pace with those guys and stay in the game. We got on a roll with the passing game."

In the third quarter, the teams traded field goals on their first possessions. At the 10-minute mark, Terry Baker pinned

Hamilton at their 3-yard line with a tremendous punt. Three plays later, Osbaldiston conceded a safety touch.

After the ensuing kickoff, Saskatchewan scrimmaged at their 33. Tim McCray ran for two before Austin hooked up with Don Narcisse on a 47-yarder to the Hamilton 28. The Cats took an interference call on the next play, and McCray crashed over from the one.

Narcisse couldn't believe his good luck. When Hamilton's defensive back Lance Shields banged up his ankle in the second quarter, Cat coach Al Bruno replaced him with a receiver, Earl Winfield. When Winfield couldn't handle the job, Bruno figured Shields on one leg was better than Winfield with two and he sent the injured player back in. Narcisse blew right by him. At the end of the third quarter, Saskatchewan had their first lead of the game, 34-30. One minute twelve later Dave Ridgway kicked a 25-yard field goal.

Starting at the 35, Mike Kerrigan fired a pass up field, which was intercepted by Glen Suitor at the Ticat 51. Kent Austin then drove the Riders toward the Hamilton goal line, where — turn about being fair play — an interception was thrown by Ray Elgaard! "We ran a reverse pass," said John Gregory. "It was a run-pass option. He should have run. It was kind of a trick play that didn't work. He threw it to the 2- or 3-yard line. The primary receiver was absolutely wide open. Ray threw it to the secondary receiver for some reason."

Twice the teams exchanged punts. At the 8:39 mark, Osbaldiston kicked a 47-yard field goal, closing the gap to four. Ten plays later, Ridgway replied with a 20-yarder of his own, making the score Saskatchewan 40, Hamilton 33, with 1:58 left in regulation time.

Starting at the 35, Mike Kerrigan threw to Lee Knight for 18 and DiPietro for 9. McAdoo ran for 6. Saskatchewan was then called for interference at their 11. McAdoo went for 2, followed by an incomplete pass. With third-and-goal, Kerrigan threw into the right side of the end zone. Tony Champion made a dazzling over-the-shoulder catch while falling to the turf. The convert was good. With 44 seconds left, the score was tied at 40.

Tim McCray fielded the kickoff at the 12-yard line and returned it to his 36. There was no thought of playing conservatively, hoping for a win in overtime.

"On the first play of that drive," said Austin, "I went to Narcisse on a stop-and-go and overthrew everybody, but that was really more to send a signal to Hamilton that they weren't going to squat on a route. I didn't feel like they could stop us. Ray Elgaard made a big second-down catch on the sidelines that kept the drive alive, and then Mark Guy came through with a big catch. On the first one over the middle, he took a good hit from the safety, but held on to the ball."

With the ball on the Hamilton 26, Austin went down on one knee to stop the clock. The teams exchanged time outs. Then, at 14:58 of the fourth quarter, before 54,088 anxious fans, the greatest moment in the history of Saskatchewan sports took place: the kick.

The snap was back. Suitor put the ball down as Ridgway moved toward it. For a split second the great domed stadium was silent. Then, as the ball flew toward the goal posts, the crowd roared. When the ball split the uprights, every Saskatchewan fan in the universe followed the ball to cloud nine.

Two seconds remained. Ridgway kicked off. Steve Jackson punted it down field to Glen Suitor who ran it out of bounds. The greatest Grey Cup of them all was over. The final score: Saskatchewan 43, Hamilton 40.

Dave Ridgway talked about the kick. "I was totally oblivious to the meaning of that kick until after the fact. Then I sat down and said, 'Holy Cow! That was a big kick!' It was an afterthought. When we got out on the field, there were two time outs and I asked my holder, Glen Suitor, to talk to me about something other than football. He got me laughing, and before I knew it, it was time to attempt the kick. I got a strange kick out of doing it. I like walking on the field in that situation and I expect to make it.

"Still, I would rather that game hadn't come down to a field goal because that's an awful lot of pressure on one person's shoulders. I just don't see living in Saskatchewan if I had missed in that situation."

Kent Austin was sensational, completing 26 of 41 passes for 474 yards and three touchdowns, winning him the Most Valuable Player Award. His performance was one of the best in Grey Cup history.

As a player, coach, or general manager, Alan Ford has been part of every Rider Grey Cup game in the modern era, except 1951. He compared the winning teams, 1966 and 1989. "I think I enjoyed 1989 more because it was for our fans. At one point, it looked like we weren't going to make the playoffs. And then, to keep battling back. Everybody in Saskatchewan identified with the team — that's the way this province is. Nothing will match the way things went in 1989."

Said John Gregory, "I was really proud for the Saskatchewan people who supported the team so strongly. It was interesting how it affected everybody, from the farmers to the meat cutters to the presidents of banks."

Indeed. After 10 years of low wheat prices, rural depopulation, crop failures, and losing football teams, winning the Cup was just what a beleaguered people needed to carry them into the last decade of the century with confidence. Winners at last. The 23-year Grey Cup drought was over.

Chapter 9
Grey Cup 1994:
B.C. vs. Baltimore

hen the Montreal Alouettes folded before the beginning of the 1987 season, the CFL went into a tailspin. Fan interest and revenues sank with each passing season. The only reason the league survived was because of spectacular Grey Cup games in 1988 and '89. In 1992, the centennial year of the Canadian Rugby Union, the forerunner of the Canadian Football League, the CFL hired former Alouette Larry Smith as commissioner. His goal was to restore the venerable league to its former days of glory. He would do so by broadening the league's financial base through expansion to the United States.

Shortly after becoming commissioner, Smith made a formal approach to the league governors about expansion south. After looking at the books, he concluded the only way for the league to survive and prosper was to find new sources of revenue in new marketplaces. New franchises would renew interest in the eight surviving Canadian cities. Despite opposition from the league's prairie heartland in Winnipeg and Regina, the governors reluctantly agreed to go with Smith's plan. They weren't happy about expansion across the 49th parallel, but no one had any other ideas.

In 1993, the Sacramento Gold Miners, owned by Fred Anderson, joined up. The Gold Miners would field a line-up comprising only Americans. Because the team had only a handful of players with CFL experience, the Gold Miners struggled through their inaugural season with a mark of 6-12. Led by Don Matthews, the winningest coach in CFL history, Baltimore joined the league the following year. Because of copyright law, they could not call the team the Colts, in hon-our of the former NFL franchise in that city. They settled on CFLs and later, Stallions. Other entries included the Las Vegas Posse and Shreveport Pirates.

The Posse, Pirates, and Gold Miners were led by men who had no Canadian football experience. Matthews had been in the league for 16 years and understood the nuances of the Canadian game: the longer and wider Canadian field, 12 rather than 11 men per side, staying five yards back from a return man before he caught a punt, a single point for punts downed in the end zone, and motion in the backfield. The biggest adjustment for Americans was the speed of the Canadian game. With only 20 seconds to put the ball into play, rather than 45 under American rules, the Canadian game seemed to go at a dizzying pace.

Matthews stacked his team with CFL veterans. It was not surprising that Baltimore was the first expansion team to challenge for the Grey Cup. After going 5-4 the first half of the season, Baltimore was 7-2 the rest of the way, finishing second in the Eastern Division. They beat Toronto and Winnipeg in the playoffs to advance to the Grey Cup against the B.C. Lions in Vancouver.

When training camp opened, the Leos, led by Dave Ritchie, were strong offensively, with Kent Austin and Danny McManus at quarterback, Cory Philpot and Sean Millington in the backfield, and a receiving corps of Darren Flutie, Yo Murphy, Matt Clark, and Ray Alexander. The offensive line, crucial to success in the '94 Grey Cup, was manned by Rob Smith, Vic Stevenson, Denny Chronopoulos, Jamie Taras, and Ian Sinclair.

The defensive secondary had been decimated by defections. The personnel guy, Bill Quinter, and Ritchie opted to rebuild it with gnarly old veterans in the twilight of their careers. They brought in 35-year-old Less Browne, and James Jefferson, Enis Jackson, and Barry Wilburn, all 31 years each. The gamble paid off, with B.C. having the second-best defence in the league. Browne led the CFL in interceptions with 11.

Although the 1994 Grey Cup would be played in the friendly confines of B.C. Place, the Lions faced the daunting task of winning two playoff games on the road in Alberta to get there. In the fourth quarter against the defending champion Edmonton Eskimos, Charles Gordon intercepted in the end zone and 40-year-old Lui Passaglia kicked the game-winning field goal with 30 seconds left on the clock. On to Calgary.

The Stampeders hadn't lost a playoff game to B.C. in 30 years. To make matters worse, the tired Lions were in no shape to play anybody, let alone the powerful Stampeders. Kent Austin had a separated shoulder, Danny McManus had torn his thigh muscle, Less Browne had a cartilage injury, and Barry Wilburn a broken rib.

But the Lions matched the Stampeders play for play in the Western Final. Calgary was leading 36-31 with a minute left, when they drove into B.C.'s end to set up for a field goal. For the first time in kicker Mark McLaughlin's CFL career, it was blocked.

With less than a minute to play, the Lions would have to move the ball 64 yards and score a touchdown to win. With Austin on the sideline, the fate of the Lions was in the hands of Danny McManus. He missed a pass to Alexander. Then he connected in the flat to Matt Clark and Yo Murphy. Darren Flutie caught one at the Calgary 4. Then it was McManus to Flutie, for the game winning touchdown. Final score B.C. 37, Calgary 36.

Because national pride was at stake, the 1994 Grey Cup was unique. It was Canada versus the United States. It was up to a battered bunch of B.C. Lions to prevent the Holy Grail of Canadian football from being spirited away to the States.

Even the Americans on the team were caught up in the nationalistic fervour. "I believe that you had to be," recalled Less Browne, the CFL's all-time interception leader. "Because you were playing on the Canadian team. That meant that Canadians all across the country were cheering for you. The whole country would be going nuts because it was the first time the U.S. and Canada were playing against each other."

Danny McManus, an American citizen said, "I don't know if it was confidence or what, but we just had a feeling we needed to represent Canada in the right way and keep the Grey Cup in Canada. We didn't want to be the first team to let the Grey Cup go south of the border."

B.C. coach Dave Ritchie agreed. "All week I'd been telling them that they did not want to be the answer to the trivia question, 'Which Canadian team lost the first Grey Cup to which American team?'"

At first, Canadian Lui Passaglia, whose CFL career would span 25 years, wasn't quite as pumped as his American colleagues. "I didn't look at it as a Canadian-American thing until afterward. But when they played the national anthem of both countries before the game, you could see it in some of the players' eyes, in their reaction to the anthems, that this was more than a Grey Cup game."

Baltimore was the jewel in the expansion crown. Don

Matthews had built his team around Americans who had enjoyed outstanding careers in the CFL. Baltimore was fourth in total offence, first in rushing, fifth in passing, and third over-all in defence. Unlike their opponents, coming into the Grey Cup, they were rested and healthy.

Mike Pringle had set records for rushing with 1972 yards and 2414 total yards from scrimmage. Tackle Shar Pourdanesh had won the Offensive Lineman Award and linebacker Matt Goodwin had been named top rookie. After the season was over, Don Matthews would win his second Coach of the Year trophy.

Baltimore's offensive line of Pourdanesh, Guy Earle, John Earle, Nick Subis, and Neal Fort averaged a whopping 306 pounds. They would face three Canadians — Doug Peterson, Dave Chaytors, and Andrew Stewart — who averaged 35 pounds less.

If football games are won in the trenches, clearly Baltimore had the advantage. They also had an outstanding quarterback in Tracy Ham, at the top of his game because Matthews — a genius with quarterbacks — believed in him and knew how to use him.

A formidable foe entered the Lions' den. A total of 55,097 fans filled B.C. Place, many carrying Canadian flags. They kept up a steady roar from the opening kickoff to the thrilling end. It was one of the best Grey Cups ever played, again a vital source of energy and renewal for the Canadian Football League.

Grey Cup 1994: B.C. vs. Baltimore

The home team struck first. After returning the opening kickoff to their 32, Kent Austin, playing with a third-degree shoulder separation, marched the Lions to the 40, where Passaglia kicked a 47-yard field goal.

On Baltimore's first play, Tracy Ham was picked off by James Jefferson. Returning the favour, Austin was intercepted three plays later by Karl Anthony. The opening quarter ended with the Lions leading 3-0.

The fireworks began with less than seven minutes left in the half. With second down at his 51, Ham completed passes down to the 11. Pringle ran for 5 yards. When Ham threw into the end zone for Armstrong, the Lions were called for interference. Ham took it in from the one.

The Lions returned the kickoff to the 35. Austin was then picked off by Ken Watson who lateralled to Anthony. Anthony ran 36 yards for a touchdown. Baltimore 14, B.C. 3. In the space of 35 seconds, the Lions went from a 3-0 lead to being down by 11.

Again B.C. scrimmaged from the 35. Austin moved them to the enemy 46 where Passaglia's punt pinned them at the 7. On second down, Ham was picked off by Charles Gordon who ran 17 yards to the end zone. Baltimore's Donald Igwebuike closed out second quarter scoring with a field goal.

With 52 seconds left in the half, Kent Austin's shoulder injury caught up with him when Watson made his second interception. After 30 minutes, Baltimore led 17-10.

The Americans had reason to be optimistic going into

the second half. They were getting lots of opportunities, and the Lions had lost their starting quarterback.

The injured Danny McManus stepped into the breach.

Early in the third quarter, it looked like Baltimore was going to pull away. They began the half with a sparkling nine-play drive culminating in a field goal and a ten-point lead. The drive took 4:34 off the clock. It was then the Lions started to implement their strategy of running the football.

And run they did.

With a first down at their 35, Philpot ran for 10 and 8 yards. Millington rambled 32 yards to Baltimore's 25; Philpot for two. Then McManus was sacked by Brigance for a four-yard loss, the only sack Baltimore got that day. Lui Passaglia came on for a 34-yard field goal try.

It was a fake! Holder Darren Flutie raced around right end for 18 crucial yards and a first down at the nine. Three plays later, McManus scored. After a drive that consumed 5:05, the Lions trailed by three. The capacity crowd could feel the momentum swing in favour of the Lions.

On B.C.'s next possession, after running every first down in the quarter, McManus switched it up, throwing to Ray Alexander for 42 yards. Philpot carried to the Baltimore 35. After an incompletion, Passaglia kicked a 42-yard field goal. The teams were tied at 20 when the third quarter came to an end.

At 3:09 of the final quarter, Passaglia booted the Lions into a three-point lead on a 27-yard field goal. But the

Americans weren't done. Tracy Ham hit Joe Washington on a 55-yarder to get the ball to the B.C. 10. After an incompletion, Ham headed for the end zone. At the one-yard mark he reached out with the pigskin to get it over the line. B.C's Tony Collier thanked him kindly and relieved him of the ball. With a face-mask penalty tacked on, the Lions scrimmaged at their 23.

But Baltimore wouldn't quit. On their next possession, set up by a great punt return and a 21-yard run by Ham, the visitors evened the score on a 29-yard field goal.

The ball changed hands four times before the Lions started from their 37 with 1:40 left in regulation time. Again the big play was a pass to Alexander, this time for 34 yards, bringing the ball to the Baltimore 36. After Millington lost two yards, Philpot gained eight. With third down at the 30, Passaglia missed a field goal from 37 yards.

Instead of conceding a single point, Mike Pringle ran it out to the two. Three plays later, Baltimore had to punt. With 28 seconds left, B.C. had a first down and a second chance on the Baltimore 34. McManus prepared to take the field for one last drive. "All we did was try to run the clock down and let Lui come on for the last play. I knew he wouldn't miss two in a row."

He didn't. David 26, Goliath 23.

Most observers were astonished at how the underdog Canadians dominated the line of scrimmage. Count Dave Ritchie among them. "I was surprised that we handled their offensive line so well," he said. "The game was won in the line. Our Canadian kids stood tall. I tell you, they stood tall. Our defensive line was as good that day as I've ever seen them play."

Danny McManus added, "We got caught up in hearing about how the American players had better coaching. I think that's what fired up our Canadian offensive linemen. It was a real battle of pride for those guys. They just stepped up to the challenge."

The proud Matthews was inconsolable. "I had a very difficult time," he said. "It took me over six months before I was able to watch the film of that game. I was very, very disappointed that we lost. I thought for sure we'd win that game."

But B.C. coach Dave Ritchie had the last word. "That whole series was just through the grace of the Lord. How else would you win the last three games on either the last play or in the last minute?"

Instead of angels in the outfield, were there seraphim in the secondary? Whatever the explanation, the symbol of Canadian football supremacy was safe for another year. The American invasion of Canada had failed.

Chapter 10
Grey Cup 1998: Calgary vs. Hamilton

"We have met the enemy and he is us."
Walt Kelly's Pogo

he pressure was building. In his first nine seasons as a head coach, 1990 to '98, Wally Buono's Calgary Stampeders finished first seven times. Stars like quarterbacks Danny Barrett, Doug Flutie, and Jeff Garcia, and receivers such as Allen Pitts and Dave Sapunjis put on the greatest displays of CFL football Calgarians had ever seen. Seven Stampeders won Most Outstanding Player Awards. Five years in a row, a Stampeder was his division's nominee for Most Outstanding Player. Forty-three Stampeders were All-Canadians. Clearly the

Calgary Stampeders of the 1990s could be included among some of the greatest football teams of all time.

And yet, they had won only one Grey Cup.

Stampeder success had been intermittent at best through the years. After their undefeated season and Grey Cup championship in 1948 and their return to the big game the following season, they missed the playoffs in eight of the next ten years. Their second golden age with stars like Terry Evanshen, Herm Harrison, Wayne Harris, and Pete Liske ran from 1960-1971, when the Stamps made post-season play in 11 out of 12 years. Still, they only won one Grey Cup in three tries.

After winning it all in 1971, the Stamps missed the playoffs for 11 of the next 15 years. Attendance fell so drastically in the early 1980s, that a "Save Our Stamps" campaign had to be launched to keep CFL football in Calgary. Close to 22,400 season tickets were sold. The club made the playoffs three of the next four years, but their coach, Lary Kuharich, alienated the fans and his players with his bizarre behaviour. Normie Kwong was the general manger at the time and, instead of hiring a high profile coach to replace the man known as Coach Q, he named assistant Wally Buono to the post. Calgary's third golden era was about to begin.

Born in Italy in 1950, Buono's family had moved to Montreal in 1953. Because his mother couldn't afford to look after Wally and his brother, the boys were put in an orphanage until she could reclaim them. After starring in high school, Buono accepted a football scholarship out west at Idaho State, even though it meant he would have to once again be separated from his mother and brother. Despite his crushing loneliness, Buono excelled at college football and was eagerly signed by his hometown Montreal Alouettes, where he enjoyed a stellar career as a linebacker and punter. Between 1972 and 1981, he appeared in five Grey Cups, winning two. He served as an assistant coach for four years in Montreal. When the Alouettes went under in the spring of '87, he headed west again, this time to Calgary, where he became an assistant coach. Three years later, general manager Norm Kwong chose Buono over more experienced coaches to turn a once-proud franchise into a winner.

In his first year at the helm, Buono's boys finished first, but lost the Western final to the Eskimos 43-23 in Calgary. Looking to 1991, Buono said, "We should be a good enough football team that we should be thinking nothing but Grey Cup because we have enough skill, depth, and talent. The players have won enough here to understand that winning is there, and that they just have to go out and get it." Although the club slipped to second that year, Danny Barrett hit Pee Wee Smith on the fly for a last-minute 68-yard pass and run for a touchdown to beat the Eskimos in the Western final in Edmonton 38-36 and send the Stampeders to their first Grey Cup appearance in 20 years and a 36-31 loss to the Toronto Argonauts.

During the off-season, stock promoter Murray Pezim, the flamboyant owner of the B.C. Lions, found himself in financial difficulty and unable to afford his quarterback Doug Flutie, who had won the 1991 Most Outstanding Player Award. He sent Flutie, centre Jamie Crysdale, and Rocco Romano to his CFL soul mate, the Stampeder's flamboyant owner and stock promoter, Larry Ryckman, trading for Danny Barrett. The deal paid immediate dividends, with Calgary finishing first and going on to only their third Grey Cup triumph in franchise history, 24-10 over Winnipeg. Flutie won his second of six Most Outstanding Player Awards.

The year 1993 was very special for the team, because they were hosting the Grey Cup for only the second time. Calgary finished first with a mark of 15-3, the most wins in team history, six points ahead of Edmonton. But on a terrible winter day at McMahon Stadium, Doug Flutie froze up in the fourth quarter and the Eskimos won 29-15 and moved into the Stampeder dressing room for Grey Cup week. Again they hosted the Western final in 1994, only to lose to the beat-up B.C. Lions on the last play of the game. Was one of the greatest teams in CFL history jinxed?

It would seem so. Halfway through the 1995 campaign, Doug Flutie had surgery on an injured elbow. But unknown back-up Jeff Garcia stepped in and didn't miss a beat, leading the red and white to their fourth straight first-place finish. The Stamps' three-year mark was 45-9, the best in CFL history. In a revamped playoff format, Calgary beat fourth-place Hamilton. Flutie returned to action, but had a terrible day. He was booed off the field. But he was sharp a week later, waxing the Eskimos 37-4 in the final. On to Regina, where the Roughriders were staging the Grey Cup for the first time.

Although the weather was beautiful all week long, a ferocious wind hit the Queen City on game day, blowing the Stampeders away and the Grey Cup back to Baltimore. For the third straight year, a great season had ended in crushing disappointment. It got worse. Flutie fled to Toronto and in 1996, again playing the Western final at home, Calgary lost 15-12 to Edmonton. In '97, they ended up second, but the prohibitive underdog Saskatchewan Roughriders rolled into McMahon Stadium and stole a close one 33-30. Wally Buono vowed 1998 would be different.

When the 1998 campaign began, Calgary was the most talented team in the country. In the past five years, that hadn't been enough. There was something missing. The 1998 Stampeders needed an attitude adjustment.

Kicker Mark McLoughlin said, "From the first day of training camp, the veterans were determined to get back to the Grey Cup and win it. We stepped forward and provided the leadership."

Overcoming injuries to 12 starters, Calgary finished first and trounced Edmonton 33-10 in the final, winning the right to face Hamilton in the Grey Cup at Winnipeg.

Calgary would face the dynamic duo that broke their hearts in 1994 and '96. As B.C. Lions, Danny McManus and Darren Flutie teamed up for the last second touchdown that eliminated the Stamps in the 1994 Western final. Two years later they did the same thing as members of the Eskimos. Their coach, Ron Lancaster, had masterminded Calgary's playoff defeat as head coach in Edmonton in 1993 and '96. When Lancaster committed the unpardonable sin of losing the Grey Cup game to Toronto that year, he found he had worn out his welcome in the Alberta capitol and moved on to Hamilton.

Calgary had been first in points and total offence, Hamilton second. Calgary yielded the second-fewest yards, Hamilton was third. Hamilton surrendered the fewest points, Calgary was second. Calgary was loaded with veterans. Fifteen had played in the '95 Cup. Only four Ticats, including kicker Paul Osbaldiston, had been in one. The Stamps would be wearing their black uniforms, in which they had never tasted defeat. They knew what it took to win a Grey Cup and how long the off-season could be when you lose.

When the Manitoba capitol first hosted the big game in 1991, fears about the weather were confirmed. At –17° C, it was the coldest Cup on record. Thankfully, 1998 saw a balmy 10° C, with a west wind of 28–37 kilometres per hour. Wally Buono addressed the troops. "We have worked awfully hard to get here," he said. "Let's not come back in here with any regrets."

On the other side, Ron Lancaster said, "We've probably got further than a lot of people thought. You've worked your tail off to get here, let's finish it off right."

Calgary won the coin toss, opting to have the wind at their backs in the second and fourth quarters.

The score after 15 minutes was 4-3 Calgary, on a McLoughlin single and field goal and a three-pointer from Osbaldiston. But Calgary opened the second quarter on the Hamilton three-yard line. Kelvin Anderson capped an 86-yard, 8-play drive with a 3-yard plunge into the end zone. The snap went awry and the convert was no good. Danny McManus replied by marching from his 24 to the enemy 13, where they had to settle for a field goal. Calgary 10, Hamilton 6.

Six plays later, Ticat Bobby Olive clearly fumbled a Tony Martino punt, but the referee blew the call. On second and 11 at the Hamilton 20, Greg Frers intercepted McManus, but was called for interference. Buono disagreed.

With passes to Flutie, Andrew Grigg, and Mike Morreale, the Cats drove to the Stamps 39. McManus then read the blitz brilliantly and hooked up with Ron Williams for a 35-yard touchdown and a 13-10 lead.

The Stamps stormed back, moving the ball to the enemy 42, where they lined up in field goal formation. Instead, holder Dave Dickenson hit Kelvin Anderson right in the breadbasket for the fake. Anderson dropped it! Osbaldiston closed out the half with a 40-yard field goal, making the score Hamilton 16, Calgary 10.

Hamilton continued to have the upper hand through the first half of the third quarter, but only came away with two points. Then Calgary's Jeff Garcia and Anderson went to work, marching 75 yards in 14 plays over seven minutes for a touchdown. Anderson had 25 yards on the ground and 15 through the air. Garcia took it in from the one on the final play of the third quarter. Hamilton 18, Calgary 17.

Calgary took the lead at 4:28 of the fourth quarter on a 22-yard field goal, set up by Aldi Henry's 26-yard interception return. McLoughlin added another three points on Calgary's next possession. With 5:45 remaining, the Stampeders were up by five.

Starting at his 35, McManus threw an incomplete pass. Then he hit Andrew to Grigg for 15. After another incompletion, McManus ran for nine and then two on a third-down quarterback sneak. He threw a short pass to Archie Amerson who took it 47 yards to the two. On third and goal, Ron Williams scored. The two-point conversion failed. Hamilton 24, Calgary 23.

There was 2:02 remaining on the clock.

"I knew as soon as we scored there was too much time left on the clock," Lancaster wryly observed.

Started at his 30, Jeff Garcia hit Aubrey Cummings for six and Travis Moore for nine. After a sneak for two yards, Garcia completed the last pass of the game to Moore for 13 yards. With 57 seconds left, Garcia ran for eight and three yards. Anderson carried two yards to the 30, Garcia to the 27. Mark McLoughlin and Dave Dickenson took to the field.

Like all great kickers, McLoughlin lived for the moment when the big game is on the line. All was silent that moment in Winnipeg, including McLoughlin and Dickenson. The ball was snapped and pinned. McLoughlin drove it through the uprights. Final score Calgary 26, Hamilton 24.

McLoughlin had been with the team throughout the Wally Buono era, experiencing the exhilarating wins and heartbreaking defeats. He had to earn the respect of his teammates and fans when he was picked to replace the enormously popular kicker J.T. Hay halfway through the 1989 campaign. His personal life had also been marked with ups and downs, from the birth of his first child in 1998 to the untimely death of his father the year before. McLoughlin struggled throughout the 1998 season to cope with his dad's death.

If Calgary had lost the 1998 Grey Cup, the Stampeders of the '90s would forever be labelled the greatest team that never was. In the weeks that followed their victory, they shared the Cup with the people of Calgary. Because of the enormous pressure to win, Grey Cup 1998 was especially meaningful for Wally Buono. "For me, it was a very satisfying win for a lot of reasons. I was happy for the players, I was happy for the organization, but I was also happy for myself."

For Winnipeg native McLoughlin, this was a bittersweet Grey Cup. "Without a doubt my dad was right by my side when I kicked it. I wish he could have been here physically to share this moment with me, but I know he was here in spirit."

Bibliography

Kelly, Graham. *The Grey Cup: A History.* Calgary: Johnson Gorman Publishers, 1998.

Kelly, Graham. *Green Grit: The Story of the Saskatchewan Roughriders.* Toronto: HarperCollins, 2001.

November 22, 2004 editions of the *Vancouver Province* and *Edmonton Journal.*

Walker, Gordon. *Grey Cup Tradition, 1987,* E.S.P. Marketing and Communications Ltd.

Acknowledgments

The author would like to thank research staff at the Regina and Calgary Public libraries, as well as everyone who has played, coached, and managed the great Canadian game.

About the Author

Graham Kelly grew up in Regina, working for the Saskatchewan Roughriders as a teenager. He covered the CFL for United Press International in Regina, 1963-68. Since 1972, he has written a weekly column on the CFL for the *Medicine Hat News*. During those years, he has covered Calgary, Saskatchewan, and Edmonton games, plus 30 Grey Cups. He has been selected to vote for the CFL All-Star teams and to be a nominator for the CFL Schlenley and League awards, as well as the Coach of the Year. In 2002, Kelly was inducted into the Canadian Football Hall of Fame, football reporters' division.

He has written three other books, *The Grey Cup: A History* and *Grey Cup Glory, The Edmonton Eskimos' 2003 Championship Season*, both published by Johnson Gorman Publishers, and *Green Grit: The Story of the Saskatchewan Roughriders*, released by HarperCollins. Kelly and his wife, Lorena, live in Medicine Hat, Alberta.

Photo Credits

Cover: CP Photo/Ryan Remiorz; Collection of Graham Kelly: page 44; Saskatchewan Sports Hall of Fame Museum: pages 64 (90.16.1), 89 (90.14).

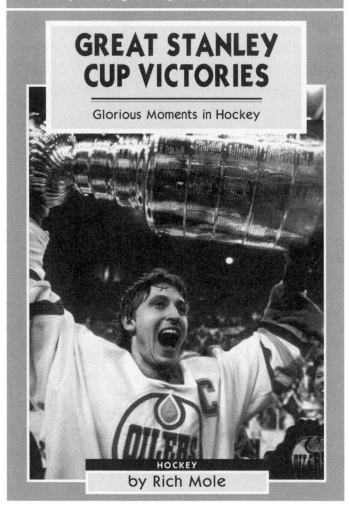

AMAZING STORIES™

GREAT STANLEY CUP VICTORIES

Glorious Moments in Hockey

HOCKEY

by Rich Mole

GREAT STANLEY CUP VICTORIES
Glorious Moments in Hockey

"Detroit's Alex Delvecchio fired a hard, low screamer that fractured Bobby Baun's right ankle. Baun was carried off on a stretcher. 'Gimme a shot,' he yelled at his doctors. In less than five minutes he was back on the ice..."

Playoffs! — The most exciting time in hockey, when the best teams battle it out for the greatest hockey prize of all: the Stanley Cup. The most thrilling and the most dramatic games are those played during the playoffs, when the stakes are high and everything is on the line. Celebrate the joy of victory with some of the greatest hockey stories of the past century.

 True stories. Truly Canadian.

ISBN 1-55153-797-4

OTHER AMAZING STORIES

These titles are available wherever you buy books. If you have trouble finding the book you want, call the Altitude order desk at **1-800-957-6888**, e-mail your request to: **orderdesk@altitudepublishing.com** or visit our Web site at **www.amazingstories.ca**

New AMAZING STORIES titles are published every month.